CÉ

EARLY SETTLEMENT

OF THE

WABASH VALLEY.

RECOLLECTIONS

OF THE

EARLY SETTLEMENT

OF THE

WABASH VALLEY.

BY SANDFORD C. COX.

BOOKS FOR LIBRARIES PRESS
FREEPORT, NEW YORK

First Published 1860
Reprinted 1970

STANDARD BOOK NUMBER:
8369-5323-1

LIBRARY OF CONGRESS CATALOG CARD NUMBER:
78-117870

PRINTED IN THE UNITED STATES OF AMERICA

PREFACE.

The favorable reception by the public of the series of articles on "Old Settlers," over the signature of "Incog." published in the Lafayette Daily Courier, during the months of October and November, 1859, has induced the writer to collect, revise, and re-publish those articles, with many others on the same subject, which have never heretofore appeared in print.

To the few Old Settlers who still remain among us, and the descendants of others who have passed from the stage of action, as well as many who have emigrated further west, this Book may contain sufficient interest to secure its perusal, and serve as a pleasant remembrancer of the "days of other years"; while the mass of our present population may be curious to know something of the character and doings of the early settlers.

AUTHOR.

INTRODUCTION.

Thirty-six years ago, at which time the historical sketches contained in this little work commence, the greater portion of Indiana was almost an entire wilderness. Its wide and tangled forests, and undisturbed prairies were the haunts of wild beasts, and the home of the wandering Indian. Only here and there were to be seen the traces of civilization. Little was then known of the country, save it was considered as one of the far-west frontiers—with but a sparse population, and that population long destined to struggle with the many hardships and privations incident to a frontier life.

The hardy boatman, as he descended the Ohio, could indeed see, peering through the dense forest, a few isolated log-cabins, and here and there a small "clearing," to use the significant language of the country and the times. But these mostly were close along the margin of the river, while back only a few miles distant, was the vast wilderness interior—still occupied by its native forest lords, whose hostile incursions were yet dreaded by the almost defenceless inhabitants. Bold and determined was the adventurer, who at that early period penetrated the western wilds, and sought in the bosom of the wilderness a sequestered home. But there were to be found those whose enterprise and daring well qualified them for the arduous task.

Kentucky and Ohio, which had but lately been settled, amid all the hardships of border life, and the alarms of savage warfare, were well prepared to furnish pioneers to subdue another wilderness. And it was only those who were inured to perils, and had often met the Indian in his ambuscade, that first pressed into the wilds of Indiana, and laid the foundation of our present happiness and prosperity. Although the first settlement of this country was not as strongly opposed by the Indians as was the settlement of Kentucky, yet nevertheless many of our hardy pioneers were made the hapless victims of savage vengeance. Although there was not in general, that open hostility and settled determination, on the part of the Indians, to maintain the soil, yet there was, if possible, a more terrible mode of warfare, which the most cautious vigilance of the settler could not guard against. Midnight massacres, and the burning of cabins over the butchered remains of the vanquished, often spread consternation throughout the border settlements, and added another vial to the just indignation of the settler against the savage marauders, who, in their turn, were frequently made to feel the fierce ban of retributive vengeance. But in proportion as the small stream of emigration gradually increased, these tragedies became less frequent, and the ruthless Indian was driven still further back into his native wilderness. The rill of emigration soon swelled into a river, which poured a strong and steady current of population into the hearts of forests which had long stood undisturbed in their sylvan magnificence, but were now doomed to bow before the leveling axe of industry. The Indians, conscious of their inability long to withstand the encroachments of the whites, who were now rapidly thronging their borders, began to think seriously of making a virtue of necessity, by selling certain portions of their domain to the United States, and thereby avoiding further difficulties, which could not result otherwise than to their disadvantage. Their propositions to dispose of their lands were readily acceded to by the government of the United States; and one treaty after another was held with the different tribes (and there were many), who for a scanty remuneration relinquished their claims to large districts of excellent land.

Scarcely were the brands of their council-fires extinguished, ere the forest resounded with the axe-man's blows, and the prolific bosom of the earth was made bare for the reception of its new occupants, who soon made the "wilderness blossom as the rose" —the smiles of Cerus to pervade the interior of vast forests, and the cheerful hum of a thrifty population to greet the ear of the astonished traveler.

How vast the change which a few years have made in the appearance, condition and prospects of Indiana? Where but lately the Indians held their war-dance, and in frightful panto-mime and in songs celebrated the heroic deeds of their forefathers or burnt the devoted captive at the stake, is now the site of a populous town, containing all the elements of wealth, comfort, and prosperity. And it may be that on the very spot where the prophet priest was wont to chant his orisons, and pour his nightly incantations on the wind, now stands a magnificent sanctuary dedicated to the worship of the true God. Splendid dwellings—temples of justice, and of learning—have taken the place of the wigwam and the gauntlet ground. Our rivers, which had long remained undisturbed, save by the Frenchman's perogue, or the Indian's bark canoe, have since become the crowded chan-nels of a vast and increasing commerce—railroads and telegraph lines have spread their net-work over the land, as our rich and varied resources have been developed, and Indiana has taken a prominent position among her sister States, and has already become one of the brightest stars in the galaxy of freedom.

CHAPTER I.

In furnishing some extracts from the Journal of the Black Creek School Master, in relation to the early settlement of the Wabash Valley, I will first give a few entries made by the young journalist while on the road moving to this country. The first memorandum of any particular interest reads thus :

FALLS OF FALL CREEK, }
MADISON CO., IND., October 24, 1824. }

Mr. Corey, the sheriff, took us in to see the Indian murderers —Bridge, Sawyer, Hudson, and John Bridge. Hudson is now under sentence of death. He sits apart from the rest, reading a small Bible. Old man Bridge, his son John, and Sawyer, are reclining on the jail floor, dressed in brown pantaloons and blue linsey hunting shirts. Hudson has on a black woolen wamus, fastened with a leathern belt. He is quite penitent, talks but little, and appears to be about forty years old,—heavy set, and inclines to be corpulent. Old man Bridge and Sawyer talked freely with father and others on the subject of their confinement. They each appear to be over fifty years of age, and are thin and cadaverous. John Bridge is an over-grown boy of about twenty,

who says his father and uncle Sawyer were the cause of his guilt.
Last night they attempted to choke him to death in prison for
disclosing their guilt—so say the guards, who relieved him from
their murderous hands.

These prisoners, with one Harper, (who escaped arrest,) in
cold blood, murdered nine friendly Indians, most of whom were
women and children, while their husbands and fathers were
absent on a hunting excursion,—cruelly shooting and stabbing
the women, and knocking out the brains of the children against
trees; concealed their dead and mangled bodies in a sink-hole
hard by, then plundered their camp of furs, deer skins, and other
valuables, which were afterwards found concealed under the floor
of Sawyer's cabin. One of the Indian women, after remaining in
the water in the clay-hole amongst the dead bodies of her slaughtered relatives for two days and nights, was taken out alive. She
said Bridge and his son, Sawyer, Harper, and Hudson were the
murderers—lived a few hours, and died.

It is thought here that Harper incited the others to participate
in the bloody tragedy. Moses Cox, clerk of the court, shot at
Harper with a rifle as he escaped precipitately down a hill.

The jail is enclosed with pickets—logs placed on end in the
ground, about sixteen feet high, forming an area around the prison
of about eight rods square, in which is a guard house, wherein
four sentinels are stationed, who keep watch day and night over
the prisoners. The sad condition of these wretched prisoners is
another melancholy proof of the truth of the scripture declaration
—"the way of the transgressor is hard."

A little brother of mine, who arrived too late to gain admittance
with the rest of us, mounted one of the pickets, climbed over the
top, and descended to the ground on the inside. A sentinel who
witnessed the dexterous feat, raised his gun and yelled, "out with
you,"—the little chap, alarmed at either the whiskers or fire-
arms of the "soger," instantly "obeyed orders," and as nimbly
as a squirrel, mounted to the top of the picket, grinned defiance
at the sentinel, and descended outside.

To-morrow we start for Crawfordsville, on Sugar river, some
sixty miles distant. We expect to cross White river near Strawtown, then take the wilderness road by Thorntown, Wisehart's,

and thence down Sugar river to the Crawfordsville settlement.

All the above named prisoners, except John Bridge, were executed on the scaffold at the Falls; he was reprieved by Governor Ray, under the gallows, after witnessing the execution of his father, and uncle Sawyer. He survived this double tragedy but a short time, and died in about a year afterward of a broken heart.

On the morning of the 25th of October, 1824, we made an early start from the Falls, and in the evening arrived at Abbott's Ford, on White river, where we encamped for the night. Next morning, the 26th, we crossed the river and took the old Straw-town road, or rather Indian trace, which emigrants had widened into a rough wagon road.

Soon after crossing the river we passed Beckworth's place. Mr. Ogle, who drove the team, told us to take a good look at that cabin, as it was the last house we would see for forty miles on our journey. This was an unwelcome announcement to the younger members of our family; but father and mother, who were inured to frontier life—having been the first white family that ever settled in Wayne county, now the most populous and wealthy county in Indiana—seemed to care but little for the hardships and privations of the wilderness.

Our ox team moved slowly along the narrow road, which wended through a vast, primeval forest, clothed in the rich drapery of Autumn. A more gorgeous and beautiful landscape I never beheld, sleeping in the golden haze of Indian Summer. But alas! how true the couplet of the song, which reads:

"We should suspect some danger nigh,
When we possess delight;"

for while I was wrapt in admiration of the beautiful scenery that surrounded me, I neglected to watch for a minute or two our flock of sheep, which brother John had placed under my especial charge, while he attempted to kill a buck. The result was, the sheep, sixteen in number, were lost. Without letting the rest know of the matter, John and myself scoured the woods on both sides of the road in search of them. In my eagerness to succeed, I wandered too far from the road and became lost! Oh, horrible! The idea of being lost in that deep wilderness, full of Indians and wild beasts, was appalling beyond description. I could hear my heart beat distinctly, and felt a dimness come over my eyes, shutting out every glimpse of the autumnal glories of the woods, which not two hours before had so enchanted me. I ran, and hallooed at the top of my voice till I was hoarse, without any response. None but those who have been lost themselves can form a correct idea of the deep, dreadful import of the word "Lost"—even in this world.

In a few hours I was found and brought back to the road, which looked more lovely to me than a bar of gold of the same width and length, though it might extend from Strawtown to the mouth of the Columbia river.

We made no further search for the sheep, but left them to the mercy of the wolves, and pursued our journey.

In the evening it grew cloudy and threatened rain. We struck camp about twilight near the road side. About eight o'clock the rain descended in torrents, accompanied by a heavy wind which roared dismally among the tree-tops, rousing us from our slumbers by its wild, deep moanings.

The weather became clear during the night, and on the morning of the 27th a white frost lay on the logs and newly fallen leaves. This morning we aimed to make an early start, but another unfortunate and unlooked for event threw our whole company into the deepest consternation. Jesse (my little brother who climbed the pickets at the Falls) followed Mr. Ogle and brother John into the woods, when they went to bring in the oxen and other cattle. Upon their discovering him following them, they told him to go back to camp, for which he immediately started, but took a wrong direction. He was not missed until we were ready to start. Imagine the panic produced when it was known he was lost! Another energetic search was immediately instituted for the lost child. The woods for miles around echoed with "Jesse! Jesse!" from more than half a dozen voices. He heard us, but supposed we were Indians, and hid in the underbrush until we got close to him, when he emerged, mounted on a log, and said: "It is quite a frosty morning"—declared he had not been lost; that he saw the smoke of the camp all the time, and heard us calling, but took us to be Indians, and was determined to make no noise nor let himself be seen until he was certain we were not Pottawatomies.

CHAPTER II.

After bringing the lost boy into camp, we soon started on our
journey. About noon we reached Cicero creek, and encamped
for dinner at an unextinguished çamp fire where some persons
had stayed the previous night. They had killed a deer, dressed
and cooked what they needed of it, and with a commendable
regard for the comfort of their fellow-travelers through the wilderness, they had salted and baked one side of the ribs of the deer
previous to leaving, and turned the other side to the fire to be
properly cooked for the next emigrants who might chance to pass
that way. We were the lucky travelers who found it, done
brown; and manna and quails to the children of Israel during
their pilgrimage through the wilderness, were not more unexpected nor acceptable, than were these cooked venison ribs to us.

After crossing the creek, we passed a fine looking horse lying
dead near the roadside. Doubtless some poor traveler had to
pack his saddle on his back for miles, or hand it over to be "toted"
by some more lucky comrade; or, it may be, some family of
movers here lost one of their best team horses, and were compelled
to pursue their journey with a weakened and less efficient team.

We drove hard to reach a stream called "Brown's Wonder"
that night, which was the only place we could obtain water before
we reached Clayroot spring, near Thorntown. The weather was
clear and warm, and the magnificent forest, clad in its variegated

robe of Autumn, was beautiful and picturesque beyond description. By the middle of the afternoon several of us began to suffer with thirst, occasioned either by partaking freely of the baked venison, or the warm weather. Search was instituted for water on both sides of the road, but none could be found except the black puddles in the horse tracks and wagon ruts. My thirst became so intense that I could not refrain from stooping down and drinking out of a horse track in the road, shutting my eyes lest I might see wigglers in the water.

Failing to reach "Brown's Wonder," we camped a few miles east of it—suffering much through the night for want of water. Early on the morning of the 28th we reached that stream, and refreshed ourselves and team with its sparkling waters. Here we met four old acquaintances from White Water, on their return from exploring the Wabash country, with which they were highly pleased. They spoke in most enthusiastic terms of the Wea, Wild Cat, and Shawnee prairies, and declared that "the Wea plain was the prettiest place this side of Heaven,"—a fact which has never been disputed by any one who ever saw it.

Among these men was Wright L——, who once basely maltreated me at school. A sight of my ancient enemy fanned afresh the smouldering embers of my wrath, and I felt like drawing him from his saddle and administering such a castigation as his former abuse of me merited; but the fact that Wright had reformed, joined church and preached sometimes, and perhaps might be a better man than he was a boy, so allayed my anger that I let him pass without any hostile demonstration on my part—although I confess I felt that I weighed something less than a ton, when I recollected that he once spit tobacco juice in my eye.

In the evening we arrived at Clayroot spring, and encamped, as well pleased as were the Israelites when Moses smote the rock at Horeb, and they had water in abundance.

The rising sun on the morning of the 29th, found us pursuing our journey. About eight o'clock A. M. we arrived at Thorntown, once a large Indian and French village, which sent its hundreds of warriors to the battle-field. It is now deserted; or, rather, its inhabitants are all absent on a hunting expedition. Wigwams composed of poles and bark cover many acres of this beautiful and salubrious plain, on which Thorntown is situated.

We soon struck Sugar river, and followed the road on its southern bank to a Mr. Wisehart's—the first house we had seen since we left Beckworth's on White river, full forty miles back. About four o'clock P. M. it turned cold and cloudy, and by the time we arrived at Kinworthy and Lee's neighborhood, it began to snow briskly.

About dark we concluded our journey by arriving in the midst of a snow storm at John Dewey's, about a mile and a half east of Crawfordsville.

I will now give a list of the early settlers of Crawfordsville and the surrounding country, made out by our journalist in the years 1824-5, &c., making but few changes from the old manuscript now before me, which reads thus:

"Crawfordsville is the only town between Terre-Haute and Fort Wayne. The land office is held here. Major Whitlock is Receiver, and Judge Dunn, Register. Major Ristine keeps tavern in a two story log house, and Jonathan Powers has a little grocery. There are two stores—Smith's, near the land office, and Isaac C. Elston's, near the tavern. Thos. M. Curry and Magnus Holmes are the only physicians, and Providence M. Curry the only lawyer in town. John Wilson is clerk of the court, and David Vance sheriff. William Nicholson carries on a tannery and shoemaker shop. Scott and Mack have cabinet shops, and George Key blows and strikes at the blacksmithing business.

Old man Hill has a small mill on the south bank of Sugar river, north of town. West of town, in the country, there is a small neighborhood composed of the following persons and their families, viz: John Beard, Isaac Beeler, three of the Millers (John, Isaac and George), Joseph Cox, John Killen, and John Stitt—who owns a little mill about two miles west of town. Southwest of town, near the Fallen Timber, live Crane, Cowen, Scott, and Burbridge. East of town resides Whitlock, Baxter, McCullough, Catterlin, and John Dewey—with whom we stopped a few weeks on our first arrival in the country. Further east is Jacob Beeler, Judge Stitt—who owns a saw mill—W. P. Ramey, McCafferty, widow Smith, and the Elmores. Zachariah Gapen has a little tan yard near Stitt's saw mill, and in the vicinity of Kinworthy and Lee's. On the north side of Sugar river, I know of but Abe Miller, Henry and Robert Nicholson, Samuel Brown, Farlow. and Harshbarger.

Besides those named, there are but few others living in the town and country. I think I am safe in saying that half a dozen more families would embrace all, including hunters and trappers, within fifty miles around.

At John Stitt's mill below town, on Sugar river, there is a fish-trap, and in one night we caught nine hundred fish, the first Spring we were in the country, most of them pike, salmon, bass, and perch. Some of the largest pike and salmon measured from two to four feet in length, and weighed from twelve to twenty-five pounds. We carried them by skiff loads and threw them alive into the mill pond hard by, which was fed by springs, and thus we had fresh fish the year round. When a customer wished to purchase a few fish, Stitt took him to the pond, and the fish were selected and the price agreed upon before the salmon was lifted from the water.

Society is in a chaotic state, but the floating elements begin to indicate some definite formations. The Baptists talk of building a small house for worship. The Rev. Hackaliah Vredenburg, of the Methodist denomination, preached here a few Sabbaths ago, and took incipient steps for the organization of a church, while the Presbyterians think strongly of building a college north-west of town, between Nathaniel Dunn's and the graveyard.

To give you some idea of the sparseness of the population at the time at which I am writing, I would state that in a difficult case of surgery, a messenger was dispatched to Terre-Haute, one hundred miles distant, through a wilderness country, for Lawrence S. Shuler, an eminent physician then residing there. After three or four days' and nights' traveling, the messenger returned with the doctor, whom he found in an adjoining county electioneering for Congress, in opposition to Ratliff Boone. After assisting Doctors Holmes, Curry, and Snyder in performing a critical surgical operation, he resumed his canvassing, was beaten, and died a few years afterward. His district extended from the Ohio river to Lake Michigan, but contained more Indians, wolves, and wild "varmints" than voters.

The Judicial Circuits were then upon the same capacious scale, but were like the young gentleman's whiskers, "extensively laid out, but thinly settled."

For many years after the time above alluded to, our Circuit Judge and lawyers had to travel from Rockville to Laporte on horseback, crossing swamps and unbridged streams through all kinds of weather, to dispense justice to the pioneer Hoosiers.

Boone's next competitor for Congressional honors was John Law. I remember hearing him and Governor James B. Ray, then a candidate for re-election, make speeches in a little half-finished frame house in Lafayette in the Summer of 1828. They both made good speeches, considering their plight at the time—having laid out on the Wea plain the previous night, without shelter or supper, and not getting their ham, eggs and coffee until about ten o'clock the next day. After the speeches were over, which were attended by most of the settlers for twenty miles around, our company returned to our canoe, and descended the Wabash to our homes.

CHAPTER III.

LAND SALES AT CRAWFORDSVILLE—VILLAGE CROWDED TO OVERFLOW-ING—SQUATTER SOVEREIGNTY RESPECTED—SPECULATORS HELD IN CHECK—LOG-CABIN HOSPITALITY—INCIPIENT GERMS OF ARISTOC-RACY—ACCESSIONS TO THE POPULATION OF CRAWFORDSVILLE, AND SURROUNDING COUNTRY—PAST-TIMES OF THE EARLY SETTLERS —LOG-ROLLING—HOUSE-RAISING—HUNTING—FISHING, &C.—WILD HOGS ON LYE CREEK AND MILL CREEK—GOING THIRTY MILES TO MILL—SUGAR BOILINGS—SINGING SCHOOLS AND WEDDINGS.

CRAWFORDSVILLE, IND., Dec. 24, 1824.

The land sales commenced here to-day, and the town is full of strangers. The eastern and southern portions of the State are strongly represented, as well as Ohio, Kentucky, Tennessee, and Pennsylvania.

There is but little bidding against each other. The settlers, or "squatters," as they are called by speculators, have arranged matters among themselves to their general satisfaction. If, upon comparing numbers, it appears that two are after the same tract of land, one asks the other what he will take to not bid against him. If neither will consent to be bought off, they then retire, and cast lots, and the lucky one enters the tract at Congress price —$1,25 per acre—and the other enters the second choice on his list.

If a speculator makes a bid, or shows a disposition to take a settler's claim from him, he soon sees the white of a score of eyes snapping at him, and at the first opportunity he crawfishes out of the crowd.

The settlers tell foreign capitalists to hold on till they enter the tracts of land they have settled upon, and that they may then pitch in—that there will be land enough—more than enough, for them all.

The land is sold in tiers of townships, beginning at the southern part of the district and continuing north until all has been offered at public sale. Then private entries can be made at $1,25 per acre, of any that has been thus publicly offered. This rule, adopted by the officers, insures great regularity in the sale; but it will keep many here for several days, who desire to purchase land in the northern portion of the district.

A few days of public sale have sufficed to relieve hundreds of their cash, but they secured their land, which will serve as a basis for their future wealth and prosperity, if they and their families use proper industry and economy, sure as "time's gentle progress makes a calf an ox."

Peter Weaver, Isaac Shelby, and Jehu Stanley stopped with us two or three nights during the sale. We were glad to see and entertain these old White Water neighbors, although we live in a cabin twelve by sixteen, and there are seven of us in the family, yet we made room for them, by covering the floor with beds—no uncommon occurrence in backwoods life. They all succeeded in getting the land they wanted without opposition. Weaver purchased at the lower end of the Wea prairie, Shelby west of the river opposite, Stanley on the north side of the Wabash, above the mouth of Indian creek, and my father on the north side of the Wea prairie.

It is a stirring, crowding time here, truly, and men are busy hunting up cousins and old acquaintances whom they have not seen for many long years. If men have ever been to the same mill, or voted at the same election precinct, though at different times, it is sufficient for them to scrape an acquaintance upon. But after all, there is a genuine backwoods, log-cabin hospitality, which is free from the affected cant, and polished deception of conventional life.

Society here at present seems almost entirely free from the taint of aristocracy—the only premonitory symptoms of that disease, most prevalent generally in old settled communities, were manifested last week, when John I. Foster bought a new pair of silver plated spurs, and T. N. Catterlin was seen walking up street with a pair of curiously embroidered gloves on his hands.

After the public sales, the accessions to the population of Crawfordsville and the surrounding country were constant and rapid.

Fresh arrivals of movers were the constant topics of conversation. New log cabins widened the limits of the town, and spread over the circumjacent country.

The reader may be curious to know how the people spent their time, and what they followed for a livelihood in those early times, in the dense forest that surrounded Crawfordsville.

I will answer for the School Master, for I was there myself. We cleared land, rolled logs, and burned brush, blazed out paths from one neighbor's cabin to another, and from one settlement to another—made and used handmills and hominy mortars—hunted deer, turkies, otter, and raccoons—caught fish, dug ginseng, hunted bees, and the like, and—lived on the fat of the land.

We read of a land of "corn and wine," and another "flowing with milk and honey;" but I rather think, in a temporal point of view, taking into the account the richness of the soil, timber, stone, wild game, and other advantages, that the Sugar creek country would come up to, if not surpass, any of them.

I once cut cord wood at $31\frac{1}{4}$ cents per cord (and walked a mile and a half, night and morning), where the first frame college was built, near Nathaniel Dunn's, northwest of town.

Prov. Curry, the lawyer, would sometimes come down and help for an hour or two at a time, by way of amusement, as there was but little or no law business in the town or country at that time.

Reader, what would you think of going from six to eight miles to help roll logs, or raise a cabin? Or from ten to thirty miles to mill, and wait three or four days and nights for your grist?—

as many had to do in the first settlement of this country. Such things were of frequent occurrence then, and there was but little grumbling about it. It was a grand sight to see the log heaps and brush piles burning in the night on a clearing of ten or fifteen acres—a Democratic torch-light procession, or a midnight march of the Sons of Malta, with their Grand Isacusus in the centre, bearing the Grand Jewel of the Order, would be nowhere in comparison with the log heaps and brush piles in a blaze!

But it may be asked, had you any social amusements, or manly past-times to recreate and enliven the dwellers in the wilderness? We had. In the social line we had our meetings and our singing schools, sugar boilings and weddings—which were as good as ever came off in any country, new or old—and if our youngsters did not "trip the light fantastic toe" under a professor of the terpsichorean art, or expert French dancing master, they had many a good hoe-down on puncheon floors, and were not annoyed by bad whisky. And as for manly sports, requiring mettle and muscle, there were lots of wild hogs running in the cat-tail swamps on Lye creek and Mill creek, and among them many large boars, that Ossian's heroes, and Homer's model soldiers, such as Achilles, Hector, and Ajax, would have delighted to have given chase to.

The boys and men of those days had quite as much sport, and made more money and health by their hunting excursions, than our city gents do now-a-days, playing chess by telegraph, where the players are more than seventy miles apart.

In my next chapter I will call the attention of the reader to the laying-off of the town of Lafayette, the organization of Tippecanoe county, the establishment of the seat of justice of said county, &c.

CHAPTER IV.

CRAWFORDSVILLE, May 27, 1825.

Robert Johnson, Esq., our new tavern keeper, has just returned
from surveying a new town on the east bank of the Wabash river,
about two miles below the trading house at Longlois, and three
or four miles below the mouth of Wild Cat creek. Mr. William
Digby, the proprietor, calls it Lafayette, in honor of the patriotic
Frenchman who periled his life and fortune for the success of the
American arms during the Revolution.

Those desirous of purchasing corner lots, can see a plat of the
new town, by calling at our recorder's office. Mr. Cowley,
recorder, or John Wilson, his deputy, will take pleasure in showing the map, and telling how near it lies to a settlement. The
proprietor thinks when a new county is laid off north of Montgomery, his town will stand a good chance of becoming the
county seat.

Mr. Johnson says the site is eligible for a fine town, although
the ground is very thickly set with hazel and plum brush, grape
vines and large forest trees, which made it difficult to survey.

Three days after laying off his town, Digby sold it to Samuel
Sargeant for the sum of $240—reserving, however, a small fraction,
the ferry privilege, and twenty acres north-east, adjoining the

town plat—which twenty acres he subsequently sold to said
Sargeant, for the sum of sixty dollars. Sargeant, who was an
enterprising down-easter, and understanding well the ways of the
world for a young man, soon hit upon a successful plan to bring
out his young town. As Crawfordsville was the all-absorbing
centre of business, civilization and every kind of enterprise for
the whole country for one hundred miles around, he thought if he
could get a few of the prominent citizens of that town interested
in Lafayette, it would be more likely to come to something. He
therefore soon struck a bargain with Isaac C. Elston, John Wilson, and Jonathan W. Powers, to whom he sold five-eighths of
all the odd-numbered lots, for the sum of $130. These new lot
holders lived at Crawfordsville, and had daily intercourse with
travelers, fortune hunters, and fortune makers, as well as with
John Beard, the people's able and popular representative, who
would of course have much to do with the laying off of the contemplated new county north of Montgomery, and the appointment
of commissioners to locate the seat of justice. But with all these
apparent advantages, Lafayette was quite languid in its infancy,
and it often became a serious question with those most interested,
whether it would live or die.

More than a year after the town was laid out, while some of
the settlers of the Wabash were attending court at Crawfordsville,
a wag jeeringly enquired: "How does your new town of 'Lay-
flat,' or 'Laugh-at,' come on? I have a mind to take a bacon
rind and go up and grease the little thing, and let the next dog
that comes along eat it." The Wabasher did not deign a reply
to this impudence, but turned off with as consequential an air as
if Crawfordsville was then a mere kitchen to Lafayette.

All that wide district of land lying north of Montgomery
county, as far as Lake Michigan, was then called Wabash county,
and was attached to Montgomery for judicial purposes. Those
who had law suits, or deeds or mortgages to be recorded, were
compelled to go to Crawfordsville to attend to such business,
until an act of the Legislature was passed and approved January
26, 1826, entitled "An Act for the formation of a new county
out of the county of Wabash, and for establishing the county
seat thereof," it was "enacted that all that part of the county of

Wabash contained in the boundaries therein specified, shall form and constitute a new county, to be known and designated by the name of Tippecanoe.''

Elston, Wilson, Powers, and Richard Johnson, as commissioner on behalf of the heirs of Samuel Sargeant (who died shortly after his sale to Elston and others), on the 4th of May, 1826, executed a title bond to the board of justices of Tippecanoe county, for all the *even* numbered lots, in a penalty of $10,000, to convey said lots to said board of justices, as a donation to said county, upon condition that the commissioners appointed by the Legislature to locate the county seat of Tippecanoe county, should locate the same permanently at the town of Lafayette.

This liberal offer of these gentlemen, with an additional donation or two by Reuben Kelsey, Robt. Alexander, and others, induced the commissioners to accept their terms, and the seat of justice for Tippecanoe county was permanently located at the town of Lafayette.

Soon after the organization of the county, the inhabitants of Tippecanoe, who were like angels visits, "few and far between,'' began to look around for suitable persons to fill the various county offices.

The sparse settlements were confined mostly to the borders of the different prairies, and along the streams. At the first election held in the county, Samuel Sargeant was elected clerk, Daniel Bugher recorder, David F. Durkee, sheriff, John Provault and William Jones associate judges, the Hon. John R. Porter being president judge. Reuben Kelsey and John Bishop were elected justices of the peace for Fairfield township, in which Lafayette is situated, and Lawrence B. Stockton was appointed by the Circuit court county surveyor.

Samuel Sargeant died shortly after his election, and Samuel Hoover was elected to fill his vacancy. Judge William Jones (father of the Hon. Mark Jones) also died soon after his election, and James Wylie was elected his successor.

If I was called upon by a lithographer for an original sketch of the town of Lafayette and its suburbs, as it was when I first saw it, I would in the first place draw the Wabash river, on a proper scale, according to Gunter, give its exact curve and meanderings, with a ferry flat, skiff, canoe, two perogues, and a keel boat, moored along its eastern bank, near the foot of **Main street**. I next would sketch three or four rude cabins, scattered along on the bank of the river, from Main street to the foot of Ferry street, where the canal packet landing now is. One of the cabins would contain Smith's store and the post office—William Smith, the store keeper, being the first post master in Lafayette; Mr. Smith was quite an enterprising, public spirited citizen, and on the arrival of the first steamboats at the Lafayette landing, was in the habit of saluting them with a "big gun," by boring a stump, charging it heavily with powder, and touching it off with a slow match, about the time the steamer was "rounding-to" to land at the foot of Main street. And often, when trade became a little dull, he would charge a stump and fire it off in order to bring in the country people to trade at his store. One morning the report of a heavy cannon was heard near the landing. The citizens of the village ran down to see the steamer. On passing Smith's store, they saw the proprietor lying upon his back on the floor, and several shelves of broken crockery and a shivered door-facing were lying smashed up around him. They picked up the prostrate merchant, who, after he partially came to himself, enquired: "Is Mouser safe? I thought I would give them a *blizzard*, but I guess I've got the worst of it. Is Mouser safe?" He then explained matters by pointing to the fragments of a large stump that stood not far from his store, which he said he charged with about a half pound of Dupont's best powder, and touched off by a slow match—that he had made a sad mistake in putting the peg that served to plug up the auger-hole on the side of the stump facing his store, and while he was peeping round the door-cheek to witness the explosion, the powder ignited, sent the plug against the door-facing in front of him, shivering it to pieces, knocking out a log of the house, smashing his crockery, and well nigh using up the proprietor. By noon the country people for many miles around flocked in to see the steamer that carried such heavy ordnance, and on learning that Mr. Smith was convalescent, and his cat Mouser safe, returned to their homes in the evening, satisfied that they were hoaxed again! Another of these cabins would be Digby's grocery; another Kelsey and Bishop's justice office; the other, Richard M. Johnson's hotel. Near the bank of the river, back of Rogers & Reynolds' present warehouse, I would draw a few large sugar trees, growing on a beautiful blue grass plat; on which I would place a large house, larger than any of those above depicted, which I would mark "Solomon Hamer's Grocery," the most public and most frequented place in the village. I would next draw "Old Sol" (not the sun, but the jolly old grocery keeper,) whom I would have standing behind the counter, handing out Mononga-Durkee whisky by the half pint to his numerous customers. On the blue grass before the grocery door, between the sugar trees and the ferry, I would draw a group of men—some pitching quoits, some hopping three hops, others wrestling, while others would be trying to get up a foot race. The hindmost man in all these sports had to pay for the liquor or take a sound drubbing, which was frequently administered in those days for the most trivial provocation. There were more black eyes, bruised noses and bit fingers in those early times, than a few. We had our Tom Hyers, Morrisseys and Benicia Boys of those days, who, frequently at our musters and general elections, would give some bloody demonstrations of their strength and pluck.

And if my lithographer would cry "more copy," I would draw Benbridge & Foster's store at the foot of Main street, where McCormick's brick warehouse is located; then I would sketch John McCormick's little one story frame store, on the corner of Main and Wabash streets, where McCormick's large three story brick block now stands, with the old veteran and his two sons, Perry and James, selling goods. Next, I would give a sketch of Joseph S. Hanna's new two story frame store house across the street south of McCormick's store (which stood where Hanna's large block now stands, on the corner occupied by J. C. Bansemer & Bro., Jay Mix and others, as wholesale grocery stores), which presented a fine appearance, being painted white, and an upper door, facing east, up Main street, being also painted white, with green stripes running up and down, and across it, in excellent taste for those early times. Taylor & Linton's store stood on the south side of Main street, where the Taylor House and Artesian bathing buildings now stand. East of McCormick's store, on the north side of Main street, I would sketch Ayres' grocery, in a little log house, situated about where Taylor & Collier's stove store now stands; William Heaton's store, in a small frame,

which stood about where O. W. Peirce's wholesale grocery house
is now situated; and Seneca & Cyrus Ball's store, in a small
frame on the corner of Main and Ohio streets, lately occupied by
Fowler & Penn. Hill & Holloway's store was kept in a little
house which stood on the ground now occupied by Ross &
Henderson's wholesale grocery establishment. Across Main
street, on the corner of Main and Ohio, Robert Johnson—formerly
of Crawfordsville, and who surveyed the original plat of Lafayette
—kept tavern in a story and a half log house, where Taylor's
large four story brick block now stands. He was a popular
landlord, had a careful and amiable wife, and an interesting
family, mostly daughters. I would then exhibit Daniel Bugher's
residence and office, a hewed log house on the corner of Columbia
and Wabash streets, where J. Ewry & Co. now keep store, and
ask for further time to complete my picture, which I expect to do
in my next chapter.

CHAPTER V.

DESCRIPTION OF THE EARLY IMPROVEMENTS IN LAFAYETTE CONTINUED
—SAMPLE'S TAN YARD—OLD COURT HOUSE—PUBLIC SQUARE COV-
ERED WITH STUMPS—A FEW STREETS AND ALLEYS CUT THROUGH
THE UNDERBRUSH—WM. S. TRIMBLE'S TAN YARD—FORD & WALK-
ER'S CORNER—A FEW RESIDENCES ON MAIN STREET—LAKE STANS-
BURY—EDWARDS' BRICK YARD—PETERSON'S TAN YARD—EXTRACT
FROM THE JOURNAL OF THE BLACK CREEK SCHOOL MASTER—MILITIA
ELECTION IN OCTOBER, 1831—DOCTOR STONE'S SPEECH AGAINST
THE STATE ACCEPTING THE GRANT OF LAND MADE BY CONGRESS
FOR THE CONSTRUCTION OF THE WABASH AND ERIE CANAL—SCHOOL
MASTER'S REPLY—A VOTE TAKEN ON THE SUBJECT—THE SCHOOL
MASTER'S TEMPERANCE PLEDGE.

In my last I left off after describing the residence and office of
Recorder Bugher, on the corner of Columbia and Wabash streets.
Next, I will draw John McCormick's small but neat residence, at
the foot of Columbia street, near the river, where the large three
story brick warehouse stands, occupied by J. M. Spencer. From
thence I will take a southeast direction, drawing a cow-path
through the underbrush towards Sample's tan yard, siuated over

the branch in the country, which is surrounded by a dense forest of large trees. Half way between McCormick's residence and Sample's tan yard, near a point on Wabash street where Temple's foundry now stands, I would draw a daguerreotype likeness of Mariam (Granny) Neff's log cabin, with the old lady seated at the window, and Polly standing in the door. The streets were then opened in patches, between houses only, and the roads and paths were cut through the brushwood and timber that covered the most of the town plat, to suit the taste of those who opened these original avenues through the brush.

My pen shall next sketch Samuel Hoover's one story frame dwelling, in which he also held the clerk's office, on Main street, north of the centre of the public square, where he afterwards erected his two-story brick block, now occupied with stores and offices.

Next, I would draw the first story of the old brick court house, which stood where the present court house now stands, surrounded by a cluster of large stumps—for the public square was originally covered with large trees. I would draw the scaffolding still standing, and Major Ferguson and his workmen laying brick; while in the back-ground I would draw Tommy Collins, a jovial old Irishman, grubbing up a large stump on the public square, where the first jail stood, near the spot occupied by the old market house.

South of the public square, near the spot where the Courier printing establishment now stands, I would draw William S. Trimble's tan yard, with the proprietor drawing hides out of a vat with a long pole, with a crooked horn on the end of it.

On the southwest corner of the square, on the corner of Columbia and Ohio streets, generally called "Ford & Walker's corner," I would place Joseph H. Martin's little frame store house, with Jacob Walker and Andrew Kennedy standing behind the counter as clerks.

On the south side of Main street, a few doors east of the square, where the Odd Fellows' new and splendid hall has been recently erected, I would place Dr. James Davis' residence and office. Next door east was John & Albert Bartholomew's store, in a little one story frame house. Further up Main street, Matthias S. Scudder lived, in a low one story frame house, and carried on the cabinet-making business on the same lot where his large brick block now stands, opposite Lahr's hotel. About a hundred yards north of Scudder's, almost hid amidst the hazel and plum brush, stood Jesse Stansbury's log cabin, on the lot where Thos. S. Cox's dwelling is situated. Near this cabin, on the east and south, was a large pond, covering, in a wet season, several acres of ground. Upon this pond, which bore the euphonious name of "Lake Stansbury," I would draw a squad of juveniles skating upon the ice, as I have often seen them, some with skates, some with shoes, and some bare-footed.

Isaac Edwards and family resided in a cabin on the hill, on the ground where the White House now stands, on the corner of Columbia and Missouri streets; and his brick yard lay east, over the bog, where John L. Reynolds has since built his beautiful frame palace, with its exquisite arbors and surroundings.

And, to complete the diagram, I would draw Matthias Peterson's tan yard, which lay back under the hill, about where Wm. Porter and B. Hart's residences stand, south and adjoining the property on which James Spears' splendid residence is situated.

Old settlers! those of you who lived here as far back as 1826-7, unroll the map of your memories, and say whether my picture is not in the main correct. I believe it will compare with the diagram imprinted on your memories long time ago.

I must now leave Lafayette, and give a brief description of the surrounding country and its inhabitants. I then will attend to events which transpired in the first settlement of Fountain county; then return through Warren county, giving a daguerreotype of old settlers and old times in Warren; and from thence to Lafayette again, and take a second view of Lafayette, in which will appear a brief allusion to the first Methodist quarterly meeting held at Lafayette, at which the renowned and eloquent John Strange officiated as presiding elder; the Black Hawk war; with a notice of a few trips up the Wabash river on steamboats, &c. As it will take some time to look over the notes and memorandums of the journalist, and arrange the names of the settlers in their proper neighborhoods, according to priority of settlement, &c., I propose to furnish the reader, by way of episode, the following extract from the "Journal of the Black Creek School Master," which reads as follows:

BLACK CREEK, Oct. 18, 1831.

No school to-day, so I will go to the militia election, and support William S—— for captain, and Gabriel B—— for lieutenant. Election organized at 10 o'clock A. M. under a shed adjoining Edward Barkley's house,—about fifteen voters present at the time of the organization. About 10½ o'clock four more voters arrived, and a tin cup of whisky was passed around. Being somewhat chilly sitting under the shed, I took a tolerable deep *nip* of it. Eleven o'clock the tin cup was passed around the second time. I touched lightly, lest I might make blunders in clerking. Felt valiant—sorry I had peremptorily declined running for captain. Noon—about thirty voters present. A two gallon jug and a bucket of water passed around with the tin cup.

A warm discussion now sprang up through the crowd. Question: "Should the State of Indiana accept the grant of land donated by Congress for the construction of the Wabash and Erie canal, from Lake Erie to the mouth of Tippecanoe river?" Doctor Stone was the most noisy against accepting the grant; his friends called him out in a speech of about twenty minutes; he spoke vehemently against the measure, and challenged opposition. The friends of the canal looked about for some one to reply. The "young school master" was chosen for that purpose. The election was adjourned to give me a chance to speak. Sorry they called upon me, for I felt about "half seas over" from the free and frequent use of the tin cup. I was puzzled to know what to do. To decline would injure me in the estimation of the neighborhood, who were generally strongly in favor of the grant; and, on the other hand, if I attempted to speak, and failed from intoxication, it would ruin me with my patrons. Soon a fence rail was slipped into the worm fence which stood near by, and a wash tub turned bottom upwards was placed upon it and the neighboring rails, about five feet from the ground, as a rostrum for me to speak from. Two or three men seized hold of me and placed me upon the stand, amidst the vociferous shouts of the friends of the canal, which were none the less loud on account of the frequent circulation of the tin and jug.

I could scarcely preserve my equilibrium, but there I was on the stand (tub) for the purpose of answering and exposing the doctor's sophistries, and an anxious auditory waiting for me to exterminate him. But, strange to say, my lips refused utterance. I saw "men as it were trees walking," and after a long and, to me, painful pause, I smote my hand upon my breast, and said, "I feel too full for utterance." (I meant of whisky—they thought of righteous indignation at the doctor's effrontery in opposing the measure under consideration.) The *ruse* worked like a charm—the crowd shouted, "let him have it." I raised my finger and pointed a moment steadily at the doctor. The audience shouted, "hit him again." Thus encouraged, I commenced the first stump speech I ever attempted to make; and, after I got my mouth to go off (and a part of the whisky, in perspiration), I had no trouble whatever, and the liquor dispelled a native timidity that otherwise, perhaps, might have embarrassed me. I occupied the tub about twenty-five minutes. The doctor, boiling over with indignation and a speech, mounted the tub and harangued us for at least thirty minutes. The "young school master" was again called for, and another speech from him, of about twenty minutes, closed the debate. A *viva voce* vote of the company was taken, which resulted in twenty-six for accepting the canal grant, and four against it. My two friends were elected captain and lieutenant, and I am back at my boarding house, ready for supper, with a slight headache. Strange none of them discovered I was intoxicated. Lucky for me they did not, or I would doubtless lose my school. I now here promise myself, on this leaf of my day-book, that *I will not drink liquor again, except given as a medical prescription.*"

Tradition says the young Black creek school master *stuck to his pledge,* and that many years after he made that entry in his day-book, he was often seen passing up and down on the packets that ran upon the Wabash and Erie canal, lecturing upon temperance, and cordially shaking hands with the old settlers, whom he found sprinkled along from Vincennes to Fort Wayne.

CHAPTER VI.

To give a full list of the old settlers of Tippecanoe county, in chronological order, would require more time, research and space than this brief sketch will allow. We propose to mention the names and localities of a few of the prominent inhabitants of the several neighborhoods, or settlements, as those neighborhoods existed shortly after the organization of the county. Many persons, equally as ancient in point of settlement, and as worthy a place in these sketches as those whose names we chronicle, must necessarily, according to the plan we have adopted, be omitted.

For the sake of system we will divide the county into four parts, thus: by running a line from Lafayette south, along the old Crawfordsville road, to the Montgomery county line, and will call the portion lying west of said line, and south of the Wabash river, division No. 1; that part of the county lying west of the Wabash river, No. 2; that part lying between the Crawfordsville road and the Lafayette and Indianapolis State road, No. 3; and the remaining portion, lying between the Lafayette and Indianapolis road, aforesaid, and Carroll county, as the line now runs, No. 4.

The residence of Peter Weaver, at the lower end of the Wea plain, shall be the beginning point. That worthy old pioneer was as extensively and as favorably known to the early inhabitants as any man on the upper Wabash. He killed more deer, wolves and rattlesnakes; caught more fish, found more bee trees, and entertained in a hospitable manner more land hunters, trappers and traders, than any other private citizen between Vincennes and the mouth of the Salimony. He is still living, in Missouri, near Keokuk, Iowa, and, although he is near one hundred years old, he still delights to hunt, fish and trap—with a success that astonishes the later generations of his sons and grandsons.

When he moved from the eastern portion of Indiana to the Wabash, he brought with him two small negro boys, named *Ben* and *Ran*, whom he had taken to raise—children of a negro woman who had been brought as a slave from North Carolina into Indiana territory, and afterwards became free by the adoption of the constitution of the State.

Slavery, even at that early day, showed symptoms of its irrepressible tendency, by unblushingly invading free territory, and putting the people to the trouble of killing it twice before it would acknowledge that it was dead.

In the Spring of 1823, while Ben and Ran were at work in a corn field at the lower end of the Wea plain, Mr. Weaver's family was startled by their cries as they made for the house, at full speed, yelling as they ran. Supposing that one of them had been bitten by a snake, a portion of the family made haste to meet them, enquiring "What's the matter? What's the matter?" They said that two men had attempted to capture them—that one of the men first tried to decoy them over the fence into the brush, to show them the road to a neighbor's house, but that before they arrived at the fence, the sight of the other man on the outside of the field, and the manner of their interlocutor, excited their suspicions, and caused them to turn and fly to the house. Such a bold attempt to kidnap the little negroes, aroused the honest indignation of the old soldier, who had marched under Washington, and he immediately repaired, with his son Patrick Henry, to the back of the field, armed in backwoods style, to reconnoitre, and, if possible, to arrest and bring to justice those who had made so flagrant an attempt upon the liberty of the unoffending boys, who were free born, and over whom he was determined the lash of the slave-driver should never fall, if he could prevent it.

Their reconnoisance convinced them that the fears of the little negroes were well founded. Signs of two men and their horses were quite plain, and portions of the ropes with which they had intended to have tied their captives, were dropped in their hasty flight; besides the neighbors had seen two suspicious looking men, answering the description of those seen by the boys, skulking through the woods near Weaver's field for several days previous.

Suspicion at once attached to an old acquaintance remaining on White Water, who at one time had an indirect claim upon the mother of the negro boys; and who, it was suspected, was concerned in spiriting away Jefferson Croker, a free negro man, whom the law had manumitted, but from his mysterious disappearance from the White Water country, it was supposed he was drawn back into slavery by the surreptitious hand of the kidnapper, when the greater portion of the freight and business of the Under-Ground railroad ran the other way.

"Jeff." as he was generally called, was a tall, well-made negro man, but not very remarkable for his intelligence. He generally made his home with Col. David Kennedy. One day when the Colonel and his family were from home, Jeff. took it into his head that he would like to see how he would look dressed in the Colonel's military uniform. So he went to the chest, took out the full suit, from the boots to the tall red and white plume that nodded in the cocked hat, and put them on himself, sash, sword, and all, and commenced promenading back and forth over the floor, contemplating himself before a large mirror, admiring his greatly improved appearance, and the figure he cut in a military suit. At times he would draw the sword out of its scabbard, and give the word of command with a truly Napoleonic air, soliloquizing as he strutted pompously across the parlor as though it was a very Campus Martius. Col. Kennedy had approached the house unobserved by the military darkie, whose manœuvres he narrowly watched through a window. Without saying a word, he suddenly opened the door and stepped into the parlor, exclaiming, "What are you doing, you black rascal, with my suit on you?" The ebony gentleman for the instant stood in silent dread—then lifting up both hands towards the Colonel,

3

imploringly said: *"'Scuse me, Massa Davy—'scuse me—I didn't go to do it!"*

Near Weaver lived Lewis Thomas, John McFarland, John Coran, Truman Rollins, Daniel Curren, Schoonovers, Huff, and old man Haines. They all owned or worked land on the lower end of the beautiful and fertile Wea plain—which for many years was regarded as the Egypt to which the people came to buy corn for fifty miles around. South-west of this neighborhood, near Clark's Point (now Pinhook), resided Samuel O. Clark, Peter Christman, Nimrod and William Taylor, Vanzandt and Abraham Morgan, John Kennedy, John W. Odell, Samuel Rankin, John Dutton, John W. and Simon Crouse, Abraham Evans, and others, in a rich, fertile, and now well-improved portion of the county. Further east and north, near Middleton (now West Point), was the Kisers, Hollingsworths, Huffs, Ewrys, Ellises, and others. The High Gap neighborhood consisted of William Dimmitt, John Bradfield, Moses Hockett, James P. Ellis, Dr. Durkee, Andrew Hoover, Sherrys, Eli Patty, and Paul and John Sheridan. On the Little Wea were the Croses, Willies, Wylies, Crouches, Brunsons, Judge Allen, Foxes, Thomas Smiley, and the Seymours. At the upper end of the Wea plain resided James and Joseph Hawkins, Baker Guest, John Provault, Wm. Jones, Joseph Fell, Wm. West, Peter Hughes, John Bear, Jno. Magill, Isaac Galbraith and Robert Sterrett. On the north side of the Wea plain lived Adam Kinser, Joseph Cox and Abel Janney; and below the town of Lafayette lived D. F. Durkee, Newberry Stockton, Edward McLaughlin, and Joseph Travis.

On the north side of the Wea plain there was a large Indian and French town, which extended from the head of the bluff below the mouth of the Wea, to where the town of Granville now stands. I heard my grandfather, who was with General Clarke when he destroyed this town in the year 1791, say, that there were at the time it was sacked, about forty shingle roof houses, occupied by French traders and mechanics, besides tents and wigwams in great numbers, which covered the ground for several miles along the prairie, on the south bank of the Wabash river. My father's farm was on the ground once covered with this Indian town. In the Fall, after the grass was burnt on the prairie, the boys of the neighborhood used to amuse themselves with hunting up the blades of butcher knives, tomahawks, brass kettles, gun barrels, &c., and the little girls in picking up beads, which in many places were strewn over the face of the ground, and had been washed by the rains into gulches along the hillside. I remember that one day my little sister and a neighbor girl came running into the cabin, exclaiming, "Is not this a rich country, when even the grass and weeds bear beads?" Each of them had a tuft of grass in their hands, on the spires of which beads were glittering, which no doubt once graced the neck of some Indian queen, or some of her maids of honor. It appeared that the blades of grass in growing had shot up through the eye of the beads, and lifted them higher and higher, in proportion to the strength and size of the weed or grass blades which protruded through the beads. I have myself found as high as six or eight Indian knives in an hour's search, soon after we moved on the farm. After the rust was taken off, these knives proved to be of excellent metal, and had not lost their temper, notwithstanding their long exposure to the prairie fires and the weather.

We will conclude our remarks on division No. 1, after alluding to the manner of conducting a militia muster, held by Capt. P. H. W., on the south side of Wea prairie, in early times. The captain was a stout built, muscular man, who stood six feet four in his boots, and weighed over two hundred pounds. When dressed in his uniform—a blue hunting shirt, fastened with a wide red sash, with epaulettes on each shoulder, his large sword fastened by his thigh, and tall plume waving in the wind—he looked like another William Wallace, or Roderick Dhu, unsheathing his claymore in defence of his country. His company consisted of about seventy men, who had reluctantly turned out to muster, to avoid paying a fine, some with guns, some with sticks, and others carrying corn stalks. The captain, who had been but recently elected, understood his business better than his men supposed he did. He intended to give them a thorough drilling, and show them that he understood the manœuvres of the military art as well as he did farming and fox hunting—the latter of which was one of his favorite amusements. After forming a hollow square, marching and countermarching, and putting them through several other evolutions, according to Scott's tactics, he commanded his men to "form a line." They partially complied, but the line was crooked. He took his sword and passed it along in front of his men, straightening the line. By the time he passed from one end of the line to the other, on casting his eye back he discovered the line presented a zig-zag and unmilitary appearance—some of the men were leaning on their guns, some on their sticks, a yard in advance of the line, and others as far in the rear. The captain's dander rose. He threw his cocked hat, feather and all, on the ground, took off his red sash and hunting shirt, and threw them with his sword upon his hat. He then rolled up his sleeves, and shouted with the voice of a stentor: *"Gentlemen! form a line, and keep it, or I will thrash the whole company!"* Instantly the whole line was as straight as an arrow. The captain was satisfied, put on his clothes again, and never had any more trouble in drilling his company.

CHAPTER VII.

LAGRANGE AND ITS PROPRIETOR—KEEL BOATS AND PEROGUES—STAPLES OF WESTERN COMMERCE, BEESWAX, FEATHERS, FUR-SKINS, WHISKY AND FEVER AND AGUE MEDICINES—INDIAN CREEK SETTLEMENT—BURNETT'S CREEK—LARGE QUANTITIES OF WILD GAME—CINCINNATUS—ITS DECLINE AND DEATH—KNIGHT, CUPPY, AND SUNDERLAND'S NEIGHBORHOOD—SETTLEMENT ON THE GRAND PRAIRIE—STROLL BY MOONLIGHT—INDIAN CREEK HILLS—VIEW OF THE WABASH RIVER AND WEA PLAIN BY MOONLIGHT—ENCHANTING SCENERY, AND DELIGHTFUL ECHOES FLOATING OVER PLAIN AND VALLEY, AND REVERBERATING AMONG THE HILLS—BARKING OF A FOX—WILD HOGS—THEIR FURIOUS ATTACK—RENCOUNTRE WITH THE HOGS—EXCESSIVE ALARM, AND IMMINENT PERIL—DELIVERANCE.

In October, 1827, Isaac Shelby, a distant relative of Governor Shelby, of Kentucky, laid out the town of Lagrange, on the lower line of Tippecanoe county, on the west side of the Wabash river. In giving a list of the old settlers in division No. 2 of Tippecanoe county, as made in my last, I will begin at Lagrange. When this town was first laid off, its proprietor considered it a hopeful rival of Lafayette, Attica, Covington, and other river towns. At first it gave fine promise of becoming a place of considerable business, and for several years kept pace with the other villages along the river. Owners and masters of keel boats and perogues, in ascending and descending the Wabash, invariably made it a point to stop at Lagrange, and exchange bacon, salt, flour, and fever and ague medicines, for beeswax, feathers, fur-skins, and whisky, in which articles the proprietor kept up a pretty active trade.

At this place there was a bloody affray between a farmer by the name of Ensley, and a boatman named Scott, under the following circumstances: Scott and a friend of his were ascending the Wabash in a perogue, heavily laden with flour, bacon, whisky, &c. Ensley, who was at Cicot's trading house, about six miles below Lagrange, asked Scott if he might ride in his perogue to Lagrange. This request was readily granted, and the three soon pushed off their little craft, and commenced ascending the river. Before reaching Lagrange there were some unpleasant feelings excited between Scott and Ensley, in regard to the management of the craft; but on an appeal to the jug, all differences were buried, and they were good friends again. After landing at Lagrange, Scott wished to cross over to the east side of the Wabash, and asked his new acquaintance if he would not ferry him over the river in Shelby's canoe, which was lying at the landing. Ensley readily assented, and the two started to cross the river. In about fifteen minutes Scott returned, and with much agitation, said: "Shelby, I have killed that man who ferried me over the river!" "Impossible! How did it happen?" enquired Shelby. Scott replied: "After he landed me on the other bank of the river, I started for Weaver's, and had not proceeded over twenty rods through the grass and willow bushes, before I was felled to the ground by a club. On looking up, I discovered that it was Ensley who had struck me, and I instantly drew a dirk and ran after him, as he made for the canoe at full speed. I overtook him before he reached the river, and stabbed him several times in the back, until he fell upon his face in the sand, where he still lies—dead enough!" Shelby said: "Let us go over and see—perhaps he is not yet dead—and you had better get him to admit how the fracas occurred before he dies, and relieve yourself from the grave charge of murder; which, in the absence of further evidence, might be fastened upon you." In a few minutes Shelby, Scott and his friend landed on the east bank of the river, and Shelby ran up to Ensley, who was lying upon his face, and eagerly enquired the number and extent of his wounds. "They are fatal! fatal!" responded the prostrate man. "How did it occur?" inquired Shelby. "Ensley, tell how it took place—tell the truth; if the man is most in the fault, say so; if you were the first to strike, say so—that justice may be done the man when you are gone, provided your wounds prove mortal." "He has killed me! he has killed me!" was all they could induce him to say. Scott, who had stood some rods distant from the prostrate man, while Shelby was examining his wounds, and interrogating him as to the manner of the fight—now spoke out and said: "You struck me first, without cause, and without my knowing you were near me, and you felled me to the ground with a club. I rose and pursued you with a knife, and struck you several blows in the back, of which you may die; but I done it in self-defence, to save my own life." Here Shelby again interposed, and told the parties to make friends and forgive each other, before Ensley entered another world. The wounded man finally relented, and said: "Scott, come here, and let us shake hands and forgive one another;" but when Scott had approached within a few yards, Ensley raised up his head, and motioned with his right hand for him to come no nearer, saying, "Depart ye cursed, I know ye not." At this Scott broke off the parley, and despatched a messenger with all possible haste for Dr. Harry L. Doubleday, who soon came, examined and dressed Ensley's wounds, which he pronounced to be extremely dangerous, directing that he should be carried home, or to Shelby's, and that he should abstain entirely from the use of spiritous liquors, which, if indulged in, might bring on inflammation and prevent his wounds from healing. Ensley was of a different opinion himself—he thought there were no hopes of his recovery, and said that he hoped his friends would allow him to enjoy the few hours remaining to him on earth in the best manner he could; and as whisky was his greatest solace, he hoped they would send off for a gallon, and let him drink of it freely, as he could not bear to be moved from the spot where he lay, and could not live longer than morning at farthest. His friends reluctantly yielded to his wishes, sent for the whisky, and built a fire near him on the sand to raise a smoke to keep off the musquitoes. Next morning the bucket of whisky was well nigh drained, and he consented to be carried to his house. In a few weeks he recovered from his wounds so as to be able to walk about, and in a few months he was sound and well. On meeting Dr. Simon Yandes, the doctor said: "Ensley, you are surely knife-proof. That time your bowels were let out by the young man you bursted the watermelon over his head in Union county, I supposed that you could not possibly recover." Ensley waived the subject by drily remarking: "I'm tough, doctor; I'm tough."

A polemic society, was organized in this town, which was strongly attended by debaters from Weaver's neighborhood east of the river, Judge Samuel B. Clark's neighborhood on the river below, and the Mace, Davis and Fenton neighborhood, in Warren county. At one time there appeared to be a strong probability of a lyceum and academy being established there. But a few cabins and small frame houses, soon brought this village to its culminating point, and it was in a few years entirely wiped out —and, like ancient Greece and Rome, it lives only in history and story.

There were in that neighborhood, besides Shelby's family, Jesse Douthit, Harvey H. Lyons, Noah Griggs, L. S. Westgate, Wm. Williams, Daniel Gooden and Immel.

Near the mouth of Indian creek was Elijah Godfrey, John Buck, William Payne, Alex. Croy, Michael Jones, Boxley and Jehu Stanley. Near Slim prairie was Enos Moore, Aaron Dawley, Fosters, Coon, Nagle and Burns. Northwest, on the edge of the Grand prairie, and in the timber lived Vannata, Eastburn, Shambaughs, Eliconhonce, McCray, Gates, Bilderbacks, Rocks, Jourdans, Pierces, Jennings, Kellogg, Rawles, and others.

North of this settlement, on the head waters of Burnett's creek, was another neighborhood, composed of several families, viz: John Clark, Elisha G. Layne, Jourdan Knight, Charles H. Marsteller, Jones Henderson, William Sims, Thomas Connelly, Newberry Stockton, Jr., Daniel Stockton, David Jones, John Barnard, James Griffith, and Lysmund Basye.

This locality was long famous for large quantities of wild game. Many an extensive deer hunt and wolf hunt has come off along the border of the Grand prairie, and in the timber about the head of Burnett's creek.

Two or three miles east of the mouth of Indian creek was another neighborhood, consisting of James Bedwell, Robert Williams, Thomas W. Trekell, William, Benjamin and Samuel Knight, Francis Sunderland, Cuppy, Starret, Suits, James Emerson, H. Oilar, Laytons, Russells, Samuel Bringham, Peter Caster, John Downey, Benjamin Crist, and others.

In this vicinity, on the Wabash river, opposite the mouth of Wea creek, D. Patton, and others, at an early day, laid off the town of Cincinnatus, which entered the list of rival river towns, with a spirit that, for awhile, promised a prosperous future. But its race was not so long or glorious as that of Lagrange; and there remains not a vestige to mark the place where the town of Cincinnatus stood.

A few miles below this defunct village I had an adventure many years ago, the recollection of which still chills my blood with horror. An account of that truly fearful adventure, I will now relate:

On a balmy evening in June, 1835, I strolled from the cabin of my brother-in-law, where I was stopping for the night, to enjoy a quiet moonlight ramble through the verdant valley that surrounded his humble mansion, which stood about midway between the Wabash river and the Indian creek hills, which lifted their elevated heads several hundred feet above the bottom lands beneath. With difficulty I climbed to the top of one of the peaks of this romantic range of hills. The scene which surrounded me was sublime and picturesque beyond description. Before me, in the distance, lay the Wabash river, rolling its silver current along the northern edge of the Wea plain, which was besprinkled with garlands of wild flowers of every rich and variegated tint. Hawthorn and wild plum bushes, overspread with wild honeysuckle and grapevine arbors grew in clusters along the river banks, as if in love with its placid, laughing waters, that flashed and flamed in the soft moonlight. I stood spell-bound, gazing upon the lovely prospect, and listening to the many voices that came floating over the prairie and river for miles distant, then reverberating and dying away in echoes amidst the surrounding hills. The talk and laughter of children, blating of sheep, barking of dogs, and gabbling of geese, for three or four miles off, came echoing around me with a clear, distinct and witching cadence. While thus enchanted with the lovely scenery which surrounded me, and just as I repeated in an audible voice,

"If there is an Elysium on earth,
It is this—it is this,"

a fox darted through the thicket, down a dark ravine, barking as it went. In a few moments back it came at full speed, and passed over the hill near where I stood. I heard a confused cracking of bushes, rattling of stones, and gnashing of teeth, with a loud boo-boo-oh, from the ravine the fox had just left. Instantly I felt the peril of my position—my hair stood on end, as the fearful truth flashed upon my mind that the fox had started up a gang of wild hogs. I ran a few yards and sprang upon a large log, which at first seemed to promise me safety, but which I soon abandoned when I discovered that I could be approached from the upper side of the hill, where the log rose but a few feet from the ground. I sprang off and ran for an oak tree that stood on the very summit of the hill, gathering from the ground, as I ran, a sugar tree limb as thick as my arm, and about eight feet long. On reaching the tree I found I could not climb it. Instantly I threw my back against the trunk of the tree, and faced my dreadful adversaries, which by this time were close upon me. I waved my club, and yelled and screamed through very fright. They made a furious onslaught—my waving bludgeon and violent gestures repelled them; they renewed the attack again and again—my whirling, well-aimed club beat back the foremost. A panorama of terrors passed through my mind, but Harpies, Furies, and the Gorgon terrors of the fabled Medusa's head, encircled with hissing snakes, would be desirable, compared with the horrible thought of being devoured alive by a gang of furious wild hogs, that would, probably, in a few seconds, rend me into a thousand pieces, crush every bone, and consume every vestige of my mutilated body, and every shred of my garments, so that none would ever know when or how I left the world. A superhuman strength seemed to nerve my arm as I plied my bludgeon, and yelled and hallooed at the top of my voice, which echoed wildly among the surrounding hills. During a slight pause in the combat, I heard my brother-in-law's voice, as he ran to the rescue, crying, "What's the matter?—what's the matter?" By the time he reached the foot of the hill, my bristly adversaries, hearing his voice in their rear, showed signs of retreating; but one old sow, who appeared to be leader of the gang, and had in her several of the devils or evil spirits that entered into her ancestors in the time of our Savior, was for keeping up the siege, which she actually did, until my brother-in-law got within a few rods with his gun, when she turned her head to one side, listened, heard his foot-falls as he ascended the hill, then raised her head, snorted a retreat, and, with her devil-possessed comrades, darted off down the dark ravine, and I felt as if an Andes had been lifted from my breast.

CHAPTER VIII.

NAMES AND RESIDENCES OF THE EARLY SETTLERS OF TIPPECANOE COUNTY CONTINUED—PRETTY PRAIRIE—PROPHET'S TOWN—BATTLE OF TIPPECANOE—MANNER OF ATTACK—DESPERATE VALOR OF THE INDIANS—INDIANS REPULSED ABOUT DAYLIGHT—COLONEL DAVIESS, SPENCER, AND OTHER AMERICAN OFFICERS KILLED—NUMBER OF KILLED AND WOUNDED—ENEMIES DISINTER THE BODIES OF OUR SOLDIERS—THEIR BONES COLLECTED AND BURIED AGAIN IN 1830 —HANNEGAN'S SPEECH ON THE OCCASION—GEN. TIPTON'S DONATION OF THIRTEEN ACRES OF GROUND WHERE THE MAIN PART OF THE BATTLE WAS FOUGHT—ENCLOSURE AROUND THE BATTLE GROUND— CONTEMPLATED MONUMENT—ROMNEY, AND ITS VICINITY—CLEVE- LAND, MONROE, FAIRFIELD, AND THEIR NEIGHBORHOODS—AMERICUS LAID OFF—HIGH PRICES OF LOTS AT THE FIRST PUBLIC SALE— PIONEER SETTLERS' OPINIONS IN REGARD TO THE FUTURE DEVELOP- MENTS OF THIS COUNTRY.

South of Tippecanoe river, on the borders of Pretty prairie, there was a settlement in early times, composed of the following families, viz: William Kendall, Moses Rush, Moots, Philip Runnels, Becker, Marquis and Samuel Starret. Further south, between Pretty prairie and Prophet's town, lived James Shaw, John Burget, Peleg Babcock, John Shaw, John Roberts, John S. Forgey, Thomas Watson, and Flemings. North of these

thinly settled neighborhoods, there was a wide, unbroken wilderness—

> "Where nothing dwelt but beasts of prey,
> Or men as fierce and wild as they."

It would be a culpable omission on my part to leave this locality without alluding to the battle of Tippecanoe, which was
fought on the morning of the 7th of November, 1811, between
Gen. Wm. H. Harrison, then Governor of Indiana territory, and
the Shawnee Prophet, who commanded the Indians in that san-
guinary engagement.

For several years previous to this battle, the renowned Shawnee chief, Tecumseh, and his prophet brother. Law-le-was-i-kaw
(loud voice), had been stirring up the various tribes of Indians
for several hundred miles around, to resist the encroachments of
the whites; advising them to make no more treaties with the pale
faces; and to prevent them surveying those tracts of land already
ceded to the whites—averring that all treaties made with isolated
tribes were utterly void—and that a valid treaty could not be
made without the joint consent and concurrence of all the various
tribes, who were but fractional portions of the one great aboriginal family.

The Prophet's forces at the battle of Tippecanoe consisted of
warriors from among the Shawnees, Wyandotts, Ottowas, Chip-
pewas, Kickapoos, Winnebagos, Sacs, Miamis, and Pottawatomies.

When Harrison arrived with his forces (consisting of about
nine hundred men) within a few miles of Prophet's town, the
Indians manifested much alarm, feigned friendship, and expressed
great surprise that their amicable feelings for the whites should
be for a moment doubted. But their friendly protestations did
not prevent the Governor from using every precautionary measure
to prevent a surprise. Guards and picket guards were stationed
around the well selected encampment the evening before the
battle, and orders were given that the soldiers should sleep on
their arms, with fixed bayonets, and their clothes on.

About two hours before daylight, the Indians made an attack
by picking off sentinels with arrows, and then rushing with
hideous yells through the lines, into the tents of the sleeping

soldiers, many of whom awoke to receive the stroke of the uplifted knife and murderous tomahawk.

Harrison and his brave soldiers met their foes, which were considered in point of numbers about equal to their own, with a firm and determined valor. Again and again were the desperate savages repulsed, in each fierce onset. Amidst the roar and blaze of musketry, and the rattle of small arms, the furious combatants were seen to grapple in the deadly conflict. Victory awhile seemed poised, then vascillating, as if in doubt on which side to alight. But with the early beams of morning the savages were driven from the field, and the almost breathless victors looked after their wounded and buried their dead comrades. In this battle about thirty-seven whites were killed, and one hundred and fifty-one wounded, of whom twenty-five afterwards died of their wounds. It is reported that thirty-eight Indians were killed on the battle field, and full as many if not more wounded, than there were of the whites. Among the killed of our gallant band, were Daviess, Spencer, Owen, Warwick, Randolph, Baen and White, while leading their heroic soldiers on the gory field, besides others, whose names and deeds are embalmed in the hearts of a grateful people. And why not? They poured out their life blood like water to protect your cradle and mine from the toma-hawk of the savages. Peace to their ashes. A few of the survivors of this glorious battle still remain among us. Let us cherish them, and the memories of the valiant dead, whose bones laid bleaching on the battle field for many years—having been disinterred by the enemy—and were gathered together and buried again by the early settlers of Tippecanoe and the surrounding counties, assisted by a few of the inhabitants of Terre Haute, Vincennes, and perhaps some other points, in the year 1830, on which occasion Hon. Edward A. Hannegan delivered an eloquent and patriotic speech, in which he eulogized the devoted heroism of the fallen brave, and their surviving companions in arms, who shared in the glory of that well-fought field, many of whom were present and listened to his entrancing eloquence.

Gen. Tipton, who was a soldier in the battle, bought the ground on which the battle was fought, and donated about thirteen acres of the ground, where the main part of the battle was fought, to the State of Indiana, as a burying place for his fallen comrades.

The battle ground is now enclosed with a good plank fence, and it is in contemplation to erect a suitable monument to commemorate the names and the deeds of those who fell on the consecrated battle field of Tippecanoe.

Resuming the order of my division of Tippecanoe county, I will begin at Columbia (now Romney), a little village laid off in August, 1832, by Josiah P. Halstead and Henry Ristine, on the Crawfordsville road, near the Montgomery county line. This will be the southwest corner of sub-division No. 3. In this vicinity lived Enos Park, John Fraley, the Talbots, John Kennedy, Martin Miller, David Martin, and others. A few miles east of Romney, James B. Johnson laid off a village in the Summer of 1832, which he named Concord. In this neighborhood resided William Brady, Daniel Travis, Daniel Stoner, Recers, Kirkindall, Johnsons, Eli Perkins, and a few others. Southeast of Concord, near Yorktown, lived the Caulkins, Wells, Coles, Trindle, Baker, Parvis, and Westlake.

On Lauramie creek, near the village of Cleveland, laid off by Hezekiah Hunter, in February, 1832, lived Alvin Pippin, James Carr, Isaac Wickersham, Stingleys, Elliotts, LaRue, Keeler, Martin Roads and James Cowley.

One or two miles southeast of Cleveland, on the road leading to Jefferson, was another village called Monroe, laid out by Wm. Major, in 1832. Here was a cluster of families, consisting of William and James H. Major, John Kilgore, Martin Lucas, Jas. B. Hartpence, Michael Culver, and a few others. I may not be entirely correct in the adjustment of these names to their exact neighborhoods, as many years have elapsed since these settlements were formed, and as they widened and extended every year, they soon became merged into one, and all the original lines of demarkation were completely effaced.

Northwest of Cleveland, in the direction of Lafayette, lived Jacob and Jasper Whetstone, William Heaton, the Kirkpatricks, Daniel Clark, Morgan Shortridge, Billings Babcock, Samuel Black, James Earl, Levi Thornton, John Hoover, Alem Breese, James Cochrane, David H. Cochran, Samuel Parsons, Matthew Orbison, Matthews, Phillip Harter, David Patton, Michael Bush, and a few others.

In naming the old settlers in division No. 4, I will begin at

Lafayette, or in its immediate vicinity, with the Grahams, L. B. Stockton, Hilt, Knapper, Aaron T. Claspill, James Thornton, Jonathan Wolf, Gushwas, Gunkle, John Doyle, James Keene, Foresmans, John Cockerell, Creeses, Walter Freeman, Silas Simpkins, Peter Longlois, John Allen, Garret Seymour, and John W. Smith.

In the vicinity of Fairfield (now Dayton), laid off by Timothy Horram as early as 1829, was Timothy Horram, William Bush, Samuel Favorite, Joseph Earton, David Pedan, Paiges, Rizers, Tooles, Samuel McGeorge, Bartimis, Strothers, Steens, Staleys, John Robinson, Jesse Evans, Cleavers, McCurdy, Vincent and William Dye, James Wylie, Christian Barr, Ward and Burkhalters.

In and about Americus, a town laid off many years ago by William Digby, on the east bank of the Wabash river, on the road leading from Lafayette to Delphi, was another neighborhood, composed of several families of the Stairs, John Cunningham, Richardson, Schoolcrafts, Stevenson, Stanfield, Gish, Benjamin Doty, and Edward Brown.

Americus was laid out on the nearest eligible ground for a town to the mouth of Tippecanoe river, where the Wabash and Erie canal was to terminate, according to the original grant of land from Congress, which induced the proprietor and many others to suppose that it was soon destined to become a great commercial town, that would throw Lafayette, Delphi, and Logansport into the shade; and the lots sold at extremely high prices. But the subsequent extension of the canal, and the hard times, combined with other circumstances, caused the growth and duration of Americus to be much after the fashion of Jonah's gourd.

I have now given you, reader, a meagre skeleton of Tippecanoe county, as it existed some twenty-eight or twenty-nine years ago, when the settlements were chiefly confined to the timber and borders of our many beautiful and fertile prairies; and along the banks of the Wabash, Wild Cat, Wea, Lauramie, Sugar creek, Buck creek, and other streams that checker and fertilize our county.

I will now leave it for the public to draw the contrast between now and then. After looking through the reversed telescope, as

I placed it in your hands to enable you to get a good view of the "day of small things;" then change the instrument, and look at things as they now are, and anticipate what they will be when the resources of our country are fully developed.

I can well recollect when we used to wonder if the youngest of us would ever live to see the day when the whole of the Wea plain would be purchased and cultivated; and our neighbors on the Shawnee, Wild Cat, and Nine Mile prairies were as short-sighted as we were, for they talked of the everlasting range they would have for their cattle and horses on those prairies—of the wild game and fish that would be sufficient for them, and their sons, and their sons' sons. But those prairies, for more than fifteen years past, have been like so many cultivated gardens, and as for venison, wild turkies and fish, they are now mostly brought from the Kankakee and the lakes.

CHAPTER IX.

EARLY SETTLERS OF FOUNTAIN COUNTY—BLACK CREEK SCHOOL MASTER'S LETTER TO HIS COUSIN BOB, DATED APRIL, 1826—CABIN WALLS COVERED WITH STRETCHED COON SKINS, MUSKRAT AND MINK SKINS—JOHN SIMPSON—HIS SUCCESS IN HUNTING—PHIN. THOMAS AND HIS YAUGER—FORKS OF COAL CREEK—OLD SETTLERS OF FOUNTAIN AND THEIR LOCALITIES—COVINGTON—JOHN EMMETT, THE PREACHER—HIS PREACHING PLACES—PARROQUETS AND SAND HILL CRANES—DEATH OF A GOOD HUNTING DOG—RUMOR OF INDIAN HOSTILITIES—GENERAL ALARM—SCOUTS SENT TO OSBORN'S PRAIRIE—PEOPLE IN FORTS—PROWESS OF MRS. R.—GUN FIRED AT THE WATERMELON PATCH—RETURN OF THE SCOUTS—FALSE ALARM—LAND HUNTER'S SCARED AT PRETTY PRAIRIE, NEAR THE MOUTH OF TIPPECANOE RIVER—SQUATTER'S RUSE—YANKEE TRICK PERPETRATED BY A HOOSIER.

In compliance with my promise made in a former chapter, that I would give a sketch of the early settlement of Fountain county, I now proceed to the task, with such data as I have been able to procure. The most authentic and reliable information I have yet found on the subject, is contained in an original letter, written by the Black creek school master to his cousin Bob, who resided in Wayne county, near Richmond, at the time he received the friendly epistle, which reads thus:

FORKS OF COAL CREEK, FOUNTAIN Co.,}
April 13, 1826. }

Dear Cousin Bob: In my last letter from Crawfordsville, I promised to give you a description of this region of country, shortly after our arrival here. I shall now attempt to redeem my promise, though I confess there is but little to write about here, except the country, which is in general in a wild, unreclaimed state, just as it came from the hands of God, and the Indians.

You recollect seeing, while on your visit to our house in Montgomery county last Spring, how the outside walls of the settlers' cabins were covered with stretched coon skins, muskrat, and mink skins, and the eaves of the houses were surmounted with buck horns, and other trophies of the chase. The same can be seen here on a more extended scale, and as fast as they become dry, the skins are taken down to make room for more.

We have in this neighborhood a blacksmith named John Simpson, a most excellent man, who is a perfect Nimrod in the hunting line. He kills more deer and turkies in one week with his old gun "Betty," than your favorite hunter, Phin. Thomas, would in a month with his yager. But it may be because game is more plenty here than in Montgomery county, where Phin. did his hunting.

It is a heavy timbered country here, and some of the settlers have a few acres apiece cleared, and under cultivation. I want father to move to the Wea prairie, on the Wabash river, where he owns prairie lands, which are much the easiest improved, but he thinks the country there entirely too new to move to, for a year or two to come. I don't see for my part how it could be much harder to get along any place than it is here; for after we are through with our day's work—clearing, making rails, or grubbing—we have to put in a good part of our evenings pounding hominy, or turning the hand mill. But it gives us a relish for our hoecake, and there is no dyspepsia amongst us.

It is very thinly settled around the Forks of Coal Creek, and, indeed, throughout this new county of Fountain. I believe I know every family around us, and as it will take but three or four lines of my letter, I will give you their names and localities:

East of the Forks live Wm. Cochran, Hiram Jones, Benjamin Kepner, and the Browns. Further up the south Fork of Coal, live Hester, Esq. Mendenhall, Wade, Peter Eastwood, Ball and Gardner. Below the Forks, in our neighborhood, live Abner Rush, Samuel Rush, John Simpson, John Fugate, Jacob Strayer, Bond, Wm. Robe, Barney Ristine, Evans, and Leonard Lloyd, a bachelor, who lives in his cabin alone, "monarch of all he surveys, and lord of the fowl and the brute," on his own premises, at least.

On the south side of the creek there are four families, namely:

Dempsey Glasscock, Joseph Glasscock, John Blair, and Patton. Down the creek is another settlement, composed of Whites, Bryants, Forbes, Medsekers, and a few more families. Up the north Fork of Coal Creek, in the vicinity of the Dotyite Mills, live Osborn, Loppe, Helmes, Jonathan Birch, and Snow.

There is quite an excitement about the location of the county seat. The lower end of the county is in favor of Covington; but folks around here prefer a more central point. The Forks here are near the geographical centre of the county, but the arguments in favor of a county seat on a navigable river, may prevent our getting the county seat located at this place.

Lest you might think there was danger of us becoming semi-barbarous in this wild region, I will here state that we have circuit preaching every four weeks, by old Father Emmett, a veteran minister of the Methodist denomination, who has been a faithful watchman on the walls of Zion for more than forty years. He is beloved by all who know him—old and young, saint and sinner. His preaching is of the plain, practical, but effective kind, that reaches the hearts of his hearers. He nas three preaching places within reach of us, viz: at John Simpson's, Kepner's school house above the Forks of Coal creek, and in White's neighborhood in the direction of Covington.

I have found two species of birds here, different from any I ever saw on White Water—the sand hill crane and parroquet. This new species of crane is quite different from the common blue crane, being much larger, and of a sandy, gray color. They go in large flocks like wild geese, but fly much higher, and their croaking notes can be distinctly heard when they are so high in the air that they cannot be seen. Parroquets are beautiful birds, and fly in flocks of from twenty to fifty in a flight. In size they are some larger than a common quail, and resemble small parrots, from which they derive their name. When full grown their plumage is green, except the neck, which is yellow, and the head red. The heads of the young ones continue yellow until they are a year old. When flying, this bird utters a shrill, but cheerful and pleasant note, and the flash of their golden and green plumage in the sunlight, has a most bewitching effect upon the beholder; who, for a moment, deems he is on the verge of a brighter sphere, where the birds wear richer plumage, and utter a sweeter song.

It is with regret that I announce to you the death of our excellent coon dog—old Bose—(the same that Sandford Catterlin and me had the fuss about, the night we cut the coon tree that fell across McCafferty's fence, above Crawfordsville.) His death, which was a violent one, was brought about in the following manner: A gang of cattle came into the sugar camp, and commenced drinking water out of the troughs. Bose was sent to drive them off. Eager as he always was to do his duty, he seized a large ox by the nose. The ox ran and jumped over a large log, dragging the dog over with it, and striking the point of the hoof of one of its fore feet on the poor dog's side, and crushing in his ribs. He lingered a few hours and died. We buried him with the honors of war, by the side of a large log. Byron's dog, that he thought so much of, and wrote such a pathetic epitaph upon, was not a better, truer dog, than poor old Bose.

I did not get the school I expected, when I wrote to you last. Col. L—— got in ahead of me.

The next Summer after writing the above letter, we find the following entry, made by our journalist:

JULY 14, 1827.

A report reached here yesterday by a messenger despatched from Osborn's prairie, that the Pottawatomie, Miami and Kickapoo Indians were massacreing the white population on Tippecanoe river near the Pretty prairie, and on Wild Cat and Wea creeks, and that they were hourly expected at Shawnee prairie, where the inhabitants were gathering into forts, and making preparations to repel their murderous attack.

We were advised that prudence dictated that our neighborhood should also fortify forthwith.

A general panic seized the people hereabouts, a majority of whom were in favor of gathering into a fort as quick as possible; but others, more used to frontier life and Indian alarms, and among them my father, thought it best to first send out a few scouts to reconnoitre and report the actual state of things. Accordingly my father, eldest brother, and Mr. R——, accompanied the messenger on his return to Osborn's neighborhood.

Without assembling together, the neighborhood awaited their return. Mother, thinking that Mrs. R——, (who was left at home with two little children during her husband's absence,) would be alarmed for her and her childrens' safety, sent her word to come down and bring her two little boys, and stay with us until her husband returned. But Mrs. R——— returned in answer to mother's kind invitation, that "she had made up her mind to stay at home and defend her house to the last extremity—that she would fight in blood shoe-mouth deep, before she would leave her cabin to be burned by the red-skins."

I thought if Mrs. R——— possessed such true grit, that I certainly had pluck enough to go into the watermelon patch and get some melons. So I told the family that I would slip out through the corn field and bring in a few melons for us to eat. Mother at first remonstrated against my going, but finally consented, on condition that I would be prudent, and keep among the growing corn, going and returning. Just as I reached the patch and was stooping to pull a melon, *bang!* went a rifle about thirty yards distant in the corn. I straightened up—clear miss, thought I; a stupid, bewildered sensation crept over me for a moment. But the thought that the enemy would soon be upon me with tomahawk and scalping-knife, dispelled the stupor that momentarily bound me, and I instantly sprang out into the growing corn and made for home with all possible speed, meeting mother about half way; she had heard the rifle, and run to the rescue without any weapon to screen me except a mother's impulsive heart.

Mrs. R——— also heard the gun, and supposed that the work of death had already commenced in the neighborhood. But her intrepid spirit was rather intensified than depressed by the proximity of danger; and her husband's axe, which she had brought in from the wood-pile, looked as though it was ready and willing to be sunk to the helve in the skulls of half a dozen Indians.

During the afternoon it was ascertained that one of our neighbors had discharged his gun at a squirrel in the field, and that he knew nothing of my being in the melon patch at the time, nor of the panic produced by the sound of his gun.

This morning our scouts returned, and brought the news that it was a false alarm; that the Indians were peaceable; that no depredations had been committed, and that the story and alarm originated in the following manner: A man who owned a claim on Tippecanoe river, near Pretty prairie, fearing that some one of the numerous land hunters that were constantly scouring the country, might enter the land he had settled upon before he could raise the money to buy it, seeing one day a cavalcade of land hunters riding in the direction of his claim, mounted his horse and darted off at full speed to meet them, swinging his hat and shouting at the top of his voice, "Indians! Indians! The woods are full of Indians, murdering and scalping all before them!"— They paused a moment, but as the terrified horseman still urged his jaded animal and cried, "Help, Longlois—Cicots, help!" they turned and fled like a troop of retreating cavalry, hastening to the thickest settlements and giving the alarm, which spread like fire among stubble, until the whole frontier region was shocked with the startling cry.

The squatter, who fabricated the story and perpetrated the false alarm, took a circuitous route and returned home that evening; and while others were busy building temporary block houses, and rubbing up their guns to meet the Indians, he was quietly gathering up money, and slipped down to Crawfordsville and entered his land, to which he returned again, chuckling in his sleeve and mentally soliloquizing—*There is a Yankee trick for you—done up by a Hoosier.*

CHAPTER X.

Another letter from the school master to his cousin has been found, which reads thus:

FORKS OF COAL CREEK, FOUNTAIN CO.,⟩
May 2, 1827. ⟩

Dear Cousin Bob: Father has sold his farm here in the woods, and talks of moving to the Wea plain. The whole family are in favor of going there, as soon as we can get ready.

Game still continues very plenty here. Last winter I stood in our door and counted twenty-two deer in a drove, skipping along within one hundred yards of the house. In a few minutes after they passed, we heard the report of a gun about a quarter of a mile distant, followed by a loud screaming, as of some person in distress. Brother Richard and a neighbor man ran to see what was the matter. They found James Simpson, eldest son of our "mighty hunter," sitting on the snow a few rods from a prostrate buck he had just brought down, twisting a cotton handkerchief around his thigh, to stop the blood in a wound he received while attempting to stick the deer. As he stooped to cut the throat of the dying animal, it gave a flounder, and turned the point of the knife into the hunter's thigh, above the knee, cutting a branch of the femoral artery, which was bleeding profusely. My brother and his assistant surgeon, discovering the extreme danger of the wound, compressed the artery by twisting a stick through a tournequet, made of a strong pair of suspenders, staunched the wound with lint and tallow from the gun box, put Jim on a temporary hand-sled constructed for the purpose, and hauled him home, leaving the slaughtered buck, which had died from loss of blood, to be devoured by the wolves—"unwept, unhonored and unsung."

We have in our neighborhood another indubitable proof of the old adage, that necessity is the mother of invention, which may be regarded as a parallel case to the one related in your story of the "choke trap."

There is a little old man named B—— in this vicinity, who is in the habit of getting drunk at every log rolling and house raising he attends, and on coming home at night makes indiscriminate war upon his wife and daughters, and everything that comes in his way.

The old lady and daughters bore with his tyranny and maudlin abuse as long as forbearance seemed to be a virtue. For awhile they adopted the doctrine of non-resistance, and would fly from the house on his approach; but they found that this only made him worse. At length they resolved to change the order of things. They held a council of war, in which it was determined that the next time he came home drunk, they would catch him and tie him hand and foot, and take him out and tie him fast to a tree, and keep him there until he got duly sober.

It was not long until they had a chance to put their decree into execution. True to their plan, when they saw him coming two of them placed themselves behind the door with ropes, and the other caught him by the wrists as he crossed the threshhold; he was instantly lassoed. A tussel ensued, but the old woman and girls fell uppermost. They made him fast with the ropes, and dragged him out towards the designated tree.

He raved, swore, remonstrated, and begged alternately, but to no effect—the laws of the Medes and Persians were not more unalterable than was their determination to punish the stubborn offender. They tied him fast to a tree and kept him there in limbo the most of the night. Nor did they untie him even after he became sober, until they extracted a promise from him that he would behave himself and keep sober for the future, and not maltreat them for the favor they had conferred upon him and themselves. Two or three applications of this mild and diluted form of lynch law, has had an admirable effect in restoring the domestic order and happiness of the family, and correcting the demeanor of the delinquent husband and father. The old woman thinks the plan they pursued far better and less expensive than it would have been if they had gone ten miles to Esquire Make-peace every few weeks, and got out a writ for an assault and battery, or warrant to keep the peace; which would cost the family, besides the trouble and expense of attending as witnesses before the justice and circuit court, ten or twenty dollars every month or two, and done no good towards reforming the old man. I reckon she is more than half right. By-the-by, Bob, I would be much obliged if in your next letter you would rehearse the story of the "choke trap," which I wish to show to Mrs. B—— and the girls, to let them see the striking coincidence in the two cases.

In compliance with the request contained in the letter, "Cousin Bob" furnished the following version of the "choke trap," an incident in the early judicature of Indiana:

During the early history of Indiana, about the year 1808, if my memory serves me correctly, in one of the neighborhoods on the east fork of White Water, there occurred a flagrant breach of the peace, which demanded a summary exercise of the "laws of the land."

A certain ungallant offender had flogged his wife in a most barbarous manner, and then drove her from home. Bleeding and weeping, the poor woman appeared before Justice Tongs for redress. The Justice wrote out an affidavit, which was signed, sworn to, and subscribed in due form, according to the then existing laws of the territory.

A warrant was soon placed in the hands of a constable, commanding him to arrest, and forthwith bring the offender before Justice Tongs, to answer to the charge preferred against him. After an absence of some five or six hours, the constable returned with the prisoner in custody. The constable, however, had a vexatious time of it, truly, for the prisoner, who was a man of giant bulk, and great muscular power, had frequently on the way, after he had consented peaceably to accompany him to the magistrate's office, stopped short and declared he would go no further—observing at the same time that neither he (the constable) nor 'Squire Tongs had any business to meddle with his domestic concerns. It was during one of those vexatious parleys—the constable coaxing and persuading, and the prisoner protesting and swinging back like an unruly ox—that the constable fortunately espied a hunter at a short distance, who was armed and accoutred in real backwoods style.

The constable beckoned to the hunter, who came up to his assistance, and who, after hearing the particulars of the affair, cocked his rifle, and soon galloped off the prisoner to the 'Squire's office.

But this was but the beginning of the trouble in the case. The witnesses were yet to be summoned and brought before the Justice—even the complaining witness had unexpectedly withdrawn from the house and premises of the Justice, and was to be looked after.

The hunter could not possibly stay long, as his comrades were to meet him at a point down ten or fifteen miles distant that evening. The prisoner was quite sullen, and it was evident that the 'Squire could not keep him safely if the constable and hunter were to leave. And although the 'Squire's jurisdiction extended from the west line of Ohio far towards the Rocky mountains, and from the Ohio river north to Green bay, yet, so sparse was the neighborhood in point of population, and so scattering were the settlers, that he and his faithful constable found that it would be of but little use to make a call upon the *posse comitatus.* But in this critical situation of affairs, the fruitful mind of the Justice hit upon a first-rate plan to keep the prisoner until the witnesses could be brought. It was simply to pry up the corner of his heavy eight railed fence, which stood hard by—make a crack two or three rails above the ground—and thrust the prisoner's head through the crack, and then take out the pry.

As soon as the 'Squire made known his plan to the company, they with one accord, resolved to adopt it. The constable immediately rolled out an empty bee-gum for a fulcrum, and applied a fence rail for a lever, up went the fence, the Justice took hold of the prisoner's arm, and, with the assisting nudges of the hunter, who brought up the rear, rifle in hand, they thrust the prisoner's head through the crack *nolens volens,* and then took out the prop. There lay the offender safe enough, his head on one side of the fence, and his body on the other. The hunter went on his way, satisfied that he had done signal service to his country—and the constable could now be spared to hunt up the witnesses.

The prisoner, in the meantime, although the crack in the fence was fully large enough for his neck without pinching, kept squirming about, and bawling out lustily, *"Choke trap! the d—l take your choke trap!"*

Toward sunset the constable returned with the witnesses. The prisoner was taken from his singular duress, and was regularly tried for his misdemeanor. He was found guilty, mulct in a fine, and, as it appeared from the evidence on the trial that the defendant had been guilty aforetime of the same offence, the Justice sentenced him to three hours' imprisonment in jail. There being no jail within one hundred miles, the constable and bystanders led the offender to the fence again—rolled up the gum, applied the rail, and thrust his head a second time through the fence. There he remained in limbo until ten o'clock that night; when, after giving security for the fine and costs, he was set at liberty, with not a few cautions that for the future he had better "let Betsy alone," or he would get another application of the law and the "choke trap."

CHAPTER XI.

ORGANIZATION OF FOUNTAIN COUNTY—PIONEER STEAMBOATS—SPIRITED RACE BETWEEN THE RIVER TOWNS—DESCRIPTION OF BACKWOODS SCHOOLS, SCHOOL HOUSES, &C.—BRANCHES TAUGHT—BOOKS, MAPS, CHARTS, &C., USED—CONTRAST BETWEEN ANCIENT AND MODERN MODE OF TEACHING.

Fountain county was organized in 1825, and soon afterward the town of Covington, situated on or near the Wabash river, was adopted as the county seat. Shortly afterward Portland was laid off at the mouth of Bear creek, and Attica near the mouth of Pine creek, on the east bank of the Wabash.

Terre Haute was the only river town of any considerable importance above old post Vincennes, and it was clearly evident from the vast body of rich lands lying on both sides of the Wabash river, recently purchased of the Indians and brought into market by the general government, that there must be at no very distant day, at least one large commercial town on the river above Terre Haute.

As yet Montezuma, Covington, Portland, Attica, Williamsport, Lagrange and Lafayette were in the chrysalis state, but were ambitious to enter the list as rivals to become the great emporium of trade on the upper Wabash.

All of them being river towns, and possessing equal, or nearly equal, natural and commercial advantages, it was hard to divine which of them would get and keep the start in the race.

Keel boats and perogues touched at all these points, and the same pioneer steamboats—Victory, Paul Pry, Daniel Boone, William Tell, Facility, Fairy Queen, Fidelity, Science, Republican, and others—stopped at the wharf of each of these towns, whenever the business of the place required it—and it was some time before the friends of either town could say their favorite was "a head and neck" ahead of the rest.

The rapid growth of Crawfordsville, which thus far outstripped all other towns in western Indiana, inspired a hope that inland towns might enter the list of competition, even against river towns, and forthwith sprung up Rob Roy, and Newtown, so near Attica, that they cramped her energies and held her back from making a fair start with the rest. Indeed, they so cut off her trade, and hopes of success, that in the spring of 1830, poor little dwarfed Attica well nigh give up the ghost. Her enfeebled and dying condition excited the pity of her sister Williamsport, across the river, who brought her over several bowls of porridge to keep her from kicking the bucket.

Whether Williamsport acted from pure motives of disinterested benevolence, or on the principle of the boy, who, when fighting, cried, "Help Jake, for help again," tradition does not inform us. My opinion is, that she acted from the prompting of a noble and generous philanthropy. Her subsequent conduct and character justifies this conclusion. I believe that Williamsport can this day (although not as large as many other towns) say, with a clear conscience,

"That mercy I to others show,
That mercy show to me."

It may not be amiss here to mention that Keep's store at Portland, and Sloan's store at Covington, furnished the most of the goods used by the people for one hundred miles up and down the river. Powder, lead, salt, iron, whisky and leather, were the staples of the trade of those days, and were exchanged for the productions of the country, such as beeswax, tallow, feathers, ginseng, furs, deer skins, wild hops, &c.

After a while Lafayette dashed ahead of all the rest, throwing dust in their faces until she got so far ahead that the dust ceased to annoy them. Portland and Lagrange, being distanced, were ruled off the track. The rest continued the race. Montezuma and Covington kept side by side several lengths behind Lafayette and Attica, which led from the scratch. Attica in running spread herself so that she threw so much dirt in Williamsport's eyes (who was so close to her), that Williamsport was compelled to fall behind, and just kept from being distanced.

The last round left only Lafayette and Attica on the track. The prize was a glittering one—bewitching and dazzling. Attica felt her inability to win it. She yielded the conquest in favor of Lafayette; nay, more, she took the sparkling diadem and placed it on the brow of Lafayette, and crowned her the *Star City of the West;* then modestly stepped back, like a bridesmaid, blushing in her beauty; she felt that she was second best, at any rate; and is now everywhere hailed as the brightest jewel on the brow of old Fountain.

Leaving Attica, I will next cross the river to Williamsport, the county seat of Warren county, and draw a daguerreotype of that town, and some of the old settlers of Warren, as far back as 1829-30.

The reader may wish to know why my peregrinations over Montgomery, Tippecanoe, Fountain and Warren counties, were so extensive in those early times? The question is very easily answered. Being a school master, I was, of course, "abroad in the land," looking up the most densely settled neighborhoods in the country; and it often took two or three of the largest neighborhoods to furnish "scholars" enough for one good school.

I should have, perhaps, at an earlier stage of my chronicles, given the reader a description of our schools in this region of country, in those early times. I now propose, with the reader's consent, to make amends for the omission by giving a brief description of backwoods schools, school houses, &c., before drawing my picture of Warren county and her pioneer settlers.

The school house, which was generally a log cabin with puncheon floor, cat-an-clay chimney, and a part of two logs chopped away on each side of the house for windows, over which greased newspapers or foolscap was pasted to admit the light, and keep out the cold. The house was generally furnished with one split bottomed chair for the teacher, and rude benches made out of slabs or puncheons for the pupils to sit upon, so arranged as to get the benefit of the huge log fire in the Winter time, and the light from the windows. To these add a broom, water bucket, and tin cup or gourd, and the furniture list will be complete.

The books then in general use, were Webster's Elementary Spelling Book, the Bible, English Reader and supplement to the same; Dillworth's and Pike's Arithmetic, Murray's English Grammar, and any History of the United States or Geography that could be procured by the parents or guardians of those who attended school. Maps, Charts, Atlases and Geographies were much more scarce than at the present day. Parents and guardians then did not have to run the gauntlet every quarter or two, to buy a new atlas, grammar, or arithmetic, to suit the taste of every new teacher that successively swayed the birch in the district, at no little pecuniary sacrifice, as well as at the destruction of all symmetry and uniformity in the intellectual training of their children. "Baker" was then spelled and pronounced the same way in all the books. And the multiplication and enumeration tables were set down in figures and diagrams just as they are now; nor have they changed a whit since I was a boy. The nine digits, and the three R's—toasted by an American Tittlebat Titmouse, as the initial letters for *Reading*, *R-iting*, and *R-ithmetic*—were then great institutions in the land as well as now. The appropriate and classic lessons contained in the text books used in those schools were indelibly impressed upon the memories of the learners, and lasted during life. Who does not remember the fable of the "old man who found a rude boy upon one of his apple trees, stealing apples"? Of the fox, that was entangled in the bramble, by the bank of the river, and came near being destroyed by flies, and when assistance was offered, declined it for the reason that a "more hungry" swarm might pounce upon him, and suck away all his blood. And the story and picture of poor dog Tray, who got severely whipped for being caught in bad company; and other like useful and instructive lessons, containing the best of morals, which loom up like mile posts along the pathway of the past. In my humble opinion, there was more system and uniformity in the education of the youth of those days than there is at the present time. The young man educated in any portion of our government, knew the elementary course of reading and studies pursued by any other, and all other students in the Union, from Maine to Louisiana, and from the shores of the Atlantic to the most remote log school house in the west, thus the better enabling the citizens of our wide-spread and common country to understand and appreciate each other; drawing lessons, and sentiments, and household words from the same books.

There were then no one hundred and one different spelling books, grammars and geographies, to bewilder and discourage the young mind with varieties, resembling Hudibras' description of conglomeration:

"An ill-baked mass of heterogeneous matter,
To form which all the devils spewed the batter."

That great improvements have been made in the art of teaching, as well as in the arts and sciences taught, within the last quarter of a century, none will deny. Mental arithmetic, the outline maps, the introduction of the black board, and mathematical and philosophical apparatus, into the schools, has greatly facilitated the acquisition of learning—rendering it easier for both teacher and student, and enabling a larger class to look upon the demonstrations exhibited in figures and diagrams, than could otherwise be made to understand the truth or fact sought to be illustrated. But the fact is equally clear, and to be regretted, that this easy and ready mode of imparting knowledge often fails to make any deep or lasting impression on the memory of the learner, who feels that he has been galloped through a multiplicity of studies, deemed necessary in the course laid down by the school or institution to which he belongs, and he finally graduates and obtains his diploma—feeling, however, that he has threaded a labyrinth through which he could not have passed without the help and side-lifts of experienced tutors—who, had they kept him much longer at his spelling and copy book, would have done him and his country far more service. Bad spelling and chicken-track chirography, are far from being creditable to a graduate of a popular college, like Dartmouth or Yale; yet we sometimes have the mortification to witness such scholastic specimens.

It was not so with those who graduated at our log school houses in the country. They were generally all good spellers, and could write a legible hand.

CHAPTER XII.

OLD SETTLERS OF WILLIAMSPORT AND SURROUNDING NEIGHBORHOODS—PINE CREEK—KICKAPOO—CICOT'S LANDING—DOCTOR YANDES AND ANOTHER MAN DROWNED—RAINSVILLE AND ITS VICINITY—REED AND DAVIS' SETTLEMENT—JACK STINSON AND THE GAMBLERS—JACK INDICTED—HIS TRIAL—HIS SPEECH—IS ACQUITTED—NATURAL SCENERY AROUND WILLIAMSPORT—THE FALLS OF FALL CREEK MINERAL SPRING BELOW TOWN—LARGE STONES ON THE SURFACE OF THE GROUND—A BOARDING HOUSE SCENE—SOMNAMBULISM—ECLIPSE OF THE SUN.

On my first visit to Williamsport, the county seat of Warren county, I stopped with William Search, who kept a boarding house on Main street, near where the Warren Republican, an excellent newspaper, is now printed and published by my old friend, Enos Canutt, Esq.

James Cunningham, the clerk and recorder of the county, boarded and kept his office in Search's house; and as the most of his time was occupied in building a couple of flat boats to carry corn to the New Orleans market the next Spring, he employed me to write in his office of nights, and on Saturdays, which would not interfere with my school hours.

The town then consisted of five families, viz: William Harrison, the proprietor of the village, who kept the ferry, and a little tavern and grocery at the foot of Main street; Dr. Jas. H. Buell, Ullery, Search, and a man called Wild Cat Wilson. Two only (Harrison and Wilson) of the families above named had children large enough to go to school. The rest of my patrons lived in the country, some two or three miles from town, and consisted of John Semans, sheriff of the county, Wesley Clark, Robb, Hickenbotham, and one or two more.

At this time Warren county was but thinly settled. Perrin Kent, county surveyor, Tillotson, Clinton, and a few other families, lived down towards Baltimore and Mound prairie.

On Redwood, and sprinkled through the woods, and on the edge of Grand prairie, lived John B. King, Shanklin, Jameson, Hall, Butterfield, Purviance, and a few others. On Kickapoo, a small stream lying north of Big Pine creek, was a settlement composed of Boggs, Enoch Farmer, Samuel Ensley, John and Joseph Cox, Seavers, the widow Mickle, McMahan, the widow Cox, Hollingsworth, Solomon Munroe, Isaac Waymire and Zachariah Cicot, a French and Indian trader, who was born on the place where he lived (near where the town of Independence now stands) more than forty years before the organization of Warren county.

It was at this place—Cicot's landing—in the Spring of 1829, if my memory serves me correctly, that Dr. Simon Yandes, with two other men, attempted to cross the Wabash river in a canoe, and were thrown out in the middle of the river, and the doctor and one other were drowned; the third with difficulty made the shore, and escaped a watery grave.

Up Pine creek, in the Rainsville neighborhood, lived James Gooden and Benjamin Crow, county commissioners, William and Jonathan Roads, Dickson Cobb, Ridinour, Seymour Roads, William Railsback, Medseker, Esq. Kearns, McCords, and a few others. Above Cicot's was Judge Samuel B. Clark, Fenton, Magee, Edward Mace (father of the Hon. Dan. Mace), Jerry Davis, John and Gabriel Reed, Thomas Johnson, Dawsons, Orrin Munson, Sino Munson, James Stewart, Moores, Bowyer and John Stevenson, *alias* "Jack Stinson," who, in his earlier and palmier days, taught school in the Reed and Davis neighborhood, and perpetrated none of the eccentricities which filled up the last twenty years of his life.

While Jack is on the tapis—the notorious "Philosopher of the Nineteenth Century," as he styled himself, with whom the most of my readers have long been acquainted. I will relate a novel triumph achieved by the "philosopher" during a term of the circuit court held at Williamsport many years since.

During the early times in this country, before books and newspapers had become plenty, some of the members of the legal profession, including sheriffs, bailiffs, &c., would occasionally engage in the very reprehensible practice of playing cards, and sometimes drink a *little* too much whisky. During a term of the court, Jack found out where these genteel sportsmen met of evenings to peruse the history of the "four kings," as they termed it. He went to the door and knocked for admission. To the question "who is there?" he answered "Jack." The insiders hesitated— he knocked and thumped importunately. At length a voice from within said: "Go away Jack; we have already *four* Jacks in our game, and we will not consent to have a "cold one" wrung in on us."

Indignant at this rebuff from gentlemen from whom he had expected kinder treatment, he wheeled off from the door, muttering vengeance, which excited no alarm in the minds of the players.

At first he started up towards the Falls to walk off his passion, if possible; but the further he went the madder he got. He finally concluded he would not "pass" while he held or might hold so many trumps in his hands; but would return and "play a strong hand" with them.

He gathered his arms full of stones, a little larger than David gathered out of the brook to throw at Goliah, and when he got near enough he showered a volley of them through the window into the room where they were playing—extinguishing their lights, the first platoon, and routing the whole band with the utmost trepidation into the street, in search of their furious assailant. Jack stood his ground, and told them that was a mere foretaste of what they might expect if they molested him in the least. Next day the pugnacious Jack was arrested to answer an indictment for malicious mischief, and failing to give bail, was lodged in jail. His prosecutors laughed through the grates of the prison as they passed. Meanwhile Jack "nursed his wrath to keep it warm," and indited a speech in his own defence. In due time he was taken before the court—the indictment read, and he was asked what he plead to the indictment. "Not guilty," he answered, in a deep, earnest tone. "Have you counsel engaged to defend you? Mr. S." enquired the Judge. "No, please your honor, I desire none; with your permission, I will speak for myself." "Very well," said the Judge. A titter ran through the crowd. After the prosecuting attorney had gone through with the evidence, and his opening remarks in the case, the prisoner arose and said: "It is a lamentable fact, well known to the court and the jury, and to all who hear me, that our county seat has for many years been infested and disgraced (especially during court time), with a knot of drunken, carousing gamblers, whose bacchanalian revels and midnight orgies disturb the quiet, and pollute the morals of our town. Shall these *nuisances* longer remain in our midst, to debauch society and lead our young men to destruction? Fully impressed with a sense of their turpitude, and my duty as a good citizen of the community in which I live, I resolved to *abate the nuisance*, which, according to the doctrine of the common law, with which your honor is familiar, I, or any other citizen, had a right to do. I have often listened with pleasure to the charges your honor gave the grand jury, to ferret out crime, and all manner of gaming in our community. I saw I had it in my power to ferret out these fellows with a volley of stones, and save the county the cost of finding and trying a half dozen indictments. Judge, I *did abate the nuisance*—and consider it one of the most meritorious acts of my life."

The prosecutor made no reply. The judge and lawyers looked at each other with a significant glance. A *nolle prosequi* was entered, Jack was acquitted, and was ever afterward considered a trump.

The natural scenery around the town of Williamsport is romantic and beautiful, well worthy the pencil of the painter or the pen of the poet. A range of hills surrounded the original town, on the north and west, crowned with amphitheatre ranges of trees, whose tops gradually rose above each other in such regular gradations, that in the Spring time, when robed in green, or when attired in their variegated hues of Autumn, they reminded one of a good, comely mother, surrounded with her bevy of lovely daughters, bedecked with green, scarlet or yellow, according to the age, taste or caprice of the wearer. A few clumps of tall evergreen pines are intermixed with these trees, along the steep cliffs that overhang the south bank of Fall Branch, a small stream that meanders through a narrow and fertile valley which lies on the north side of town. This little stream takes its name from a cataract, where its pellucid waters are precipitated over falls some eighty or one hundred feet high, into a deep chasm, resembling the deep, narrow bed of the Niagara river, which is born of the most stupendous and sublime cataract in the world. Near the falls is a deep chasm, or fissure in the earth, produced no doubt by an earthquake, or some great convulsion of nature, along which pedestrians can walk single file, from the top of the hill through this subterranean passage to the foot of the falls. Any person fond of the marvelous, or desirous of being reminded of the dark valley of the shadow of death, can gratify their curiosity by taking a lonely ramble down this dark, deep descent. This cataract and chasm are near the railroad depot, northwest of town. The interest of this little Niagara is greatly enhanced during the Spring and Winter freshets, when the accumulated waters of Fall Branch leap and thunder over the rocks, throwing up foam and spray that forms a mimic rainbow above the heads of the aquatic shrubs and bushes that line the banks of the noisy streamlet, which laughs and leaps along in the sunlight a few hundred yards, until it is lost in the placid bosom of the Wabash river, which rolls its broad, clear current along the eastern margin of the town. At the Falls, and in the hills around the town, is to be found some of the best sand and free stone in the State. A few huge specimens, about the size of an ordinary court house, can be seen lying around on the surface of the ground in several places, near the town, as if nature had placed them there to direct the attention of man to the rich quarries that lie imbedded beneath. About half a mile below town, surrounded by a broken and romantic landscape, is a large mineral spring, whose chalybeate waters are but little inferior to the celebrated artesian well at Lafayette, which is fast becoming a popular watering place for invalids and excursionists.

An incident occurred while I was boarding with Search in Williamsport, in the Winter of 1830, which occasioned no little vexation to the landlord and myself, as well as not a little merriment to the other boarders and inmates of the house. From childhood I had been subject to walking in my sleep. When from home, I always made it a point to get a bed to myself, if possible, but never made mention of my somnambulistic predisposition to any one. It so happened one night, that our boarding house was so crowded with lodgers that, to give all comfortable beds, it was so arranged that the landlady took the three children in bed with her, and mine host was to lodge that night in bed with me—who had always a bed to myself exclusively. This arrangement was made, however, entirely without my knowledge, as I had retired to rest early that night, and was far in the land of dreams before Search got into bed with me. Whether he touched me in getting into bed, or the simple stirring of the bed clothes disturbed me, I cannot say; but sure it was, "a change came o'er the spirit of my dream" from the moment he planted himself in bed by my side. I began to dream of a large, two-fisted antagonist, approaching me in a menacing manner—drawing nearer and nearer with clenched fist, and uplifted arm, while his piercing black eyes held a steady and fiend-like gaze upon me. I thought now was my time if I struck the first blow; so I let drive with all my might and hit my sleeping bed-fellow plumb in the eye. A hound kicked in the ribs would not have set up a more piteous howl than did my friend Search. His mingled cries and groans startled every sleeper in the house, who simultaneously sprang upon the floor, crying "What's the matter?" "Oh! he has ruined me! he has put out my eye—bursted the ball!" If old Polyphemus, when Ulysses put out his eye with a sharpened shaft of pine, roared louder than mine host did on this occasion, it was because he was bigger and had stronger lungs. A light was instantly struck—the camphor bottle was hurriedly brought —the unfortunate Search was taken from the bed and placed on a chair by the fire—his eye examined, and his forehead bathed with camphor. Cunningham and Ritchey decided the eye was not put out, but was badly bruised; and advised that a rotten apple be applied immediately, to prevent the eye turning black. At this stage of proceeding, I yawned, and affected to wake up—enquired what was the matter, and on being told I expressed my surprise, and unfeigned regret, for what had happened. Rotten apple was bound over his eye, and in about an hour all returned to their beds. Search crawled into bed with his wife and children for the remainder of the night; and I had the whole of the bed to myself. During the night the rotten apple slipped from his eye, which in the morning showed a partial eclipse—and in the evening the eclipse was almost total—and a black ring encircled his blood-shot eye for at least a week. At breakfast I repeated my regrets, and apologized in the best manner I could. Little was then said to increase my mortification, or make light of the landlord's misfortune. But before a week passed, the boarders made frequent allusions to the great eclipse of the sun, which was to take place in a few weeks, and thought that other little eclipse might be regarded as a precursor of the larger that was to follow, to call our attention to the almanac, that we might have our pieces of smoked glass ready to gaze at the sublime spectacle when it made its appearance.

CHAPTER XIII.

OLD SETTLERS OF CLINTON COUNTY—TWELVE MILE PRAIRIE—JEFFER-SON, FRANKFORT, AND MICHIGAN LAID OFF—ELECTION OF COUNTY OFFICERS—FIRST RELIGIOUS MEETING HELD ON THE TWELVE MILE PRAIRIE—ADVENTURE WITH A SUPPOSED ROBBER IN THE WILDER-NESS.

Clinton county contains 432 square miles. It was organized in 1830. Its principal streams are the middle and south forks of Wild Cat, Sugar, and some smaller creeks. Its rich and fertile soil is well timbered, with the exception of that portion known as the Twelve Mile prairie, the borders of which contained the first settlements made in the county. Nathan Kirk settled near its east end, and William Clark near its west end, as early as the year 1827, and their houses were stopping places for travelers, Indian traders, and land hunters for many years.

It may not be uninteresting to give here a list of the old settlers who resided in Clinton county at the close of the year 1828, as furnished by one of the number, in whose statements implicit confidence may be placed. Add to the names of Kirk and William Clark, those of Mordicai, McKinsey, Robert Dunn, William Hodgen, John Bunton, Moses Brockman, Eli Armintrout (to whom I am indebted for valuable data relating to the early inhabitants of Clinton county), David Clark, Elijah Rodgers, Peter Graves, Zabina Babcock, John Ross, David Kilgore, Joseph Hill, Charles Usher, George Michael, John Douglass, John B. Douglass, Isaac D. Armstrong, Matthew Bunnell, Noah Bunnell, Col. William Douglass, John Allen, James Allen, Maj. John Brown, Samuel McQueen, Samuel Thompson, Elkana Timmons, John, William and Nicholas Pence, and Christian Good.

The town of Jefferson was laid off by David Kilgore, in 1830. L. B. Stockton surveyed the plat, Clinton then being attached to Tippecanoe county for judicial purposes.

An election for clerk, recorder, and commissioners of the county was held at Jefferson, in April, 1830, on which occasion Samuel D. Maxwell (now Mayor of the city of Indianapolis) was elected clerk, Beal Dorsey recorder, and Joseph Hill, Mordecai McKinsey, and John Douglass county commissioners. On the 15th day of May, 1830, the county seat was located at the town of Frankfort, where it has ever since remained.

The following September the town of Michigan was laid off by Joseph Hill and Robert Edwards.

At the August election in 1830, William Douglass was elected probate judge, and Samuel Mitchell and John Ross associate judges. Solomon Young and Perry S. Timmons received an equal number of votes for the office of sheriff; lots were cast, and Young succeeded in getting the office.

The Indians were quite plenty for several years after the first settlement of the county—the Twelve Mile prairie being a resort for hunting parties of various tribes until 1830–31.

The first sermon preached in the county was delivered at the cabin of David Clark, on the Twelve Mile prairie, in 1828, by a local Methodist preacher, named Joel Dolby, who was working for Clark at the time; and it was said that he split his thousand rails a day, out of timber that was drawn into the prairie in line for a fence. It was a novel and refreshing sight to see the people flocking in from every direction for eight or ten miles around, to hear this laborious man of God proclaim the everlasting gospel to the dwellers in the wilderness, many of whom had not heard a sermon for several long years before. Some families came in ox-carts, some in wagons drawn by horses, and others on foot.

There was then no waste of perfumery, nor patent leather. People then looked more to the useful and substantial than to display. Cigars and brandy had not then enamored the fast young men of our largest towns, much less the rural population of backwoods Clinton.

While making mention of the Twelve Mile prairie and its early settlers, it reminds me of an incident which a young friend of mine related to me on his return from Eaton, Ohio, during the Summer of 1838, which I will give as nearly in the words of the narrator as possible: "I left Lafayette after breakfast, with a single horse and buggy, carrying my saddle and riding bridle with me in the buggy, to use in case I might need them on the road, or after arriving in Ohio. I drove leisurely, and stopped at Sims' store in Jefferson, Clinton county, and wrote a letter back containing some business directions I had forgotten to give before leaving in the morning. During my short stay in the store, various customers passed in and out, as usual, and among them were two or three suspicious looking individuals, who examined my horse and buggy as closely as if they contemplated buying them. Of their conduct, however, I thought but little until the next morning. Soon after I left Shoemaker's tavern, which stood near the middle of the Twelve Mile prairie, I overtook a young man dressed in a blue surtout cloth coat, black pants and white hat, riding a fine looking bay mare, apparently five or six years old. After passing the ordinary salutations, he asked me if I was traveling far on that road. I replied that I expected to go beyond Indianapolis. He said we would be company—that he was going to Ohio, and as he had never traveled the road before, he was glad to fall in with company. I was surprised at this announcement, for I supposed he lived in the neighborhood, as he carried no port-manteau, overcoat, nor umbrella, had no girth to his saddle, nor were there any shoes on the animal he was riding. There was nothing about himself nor the beast he was riding, that indicated travel. I thought at times that he looked like one of the young men I saw in Jefferson the previous evening. He denied, however, being there when I passed through, and said he had stayed all night with an old acquaintance a few miles east of that town. We had not proceeded over a mile or two together until we overtook an old acquaintance of mine, who lived in the neighborhood, walking the same direction we were traveling. I invited him to ride with me in the buggy, and he readily accepted my invitation. The first private opportunity he had, he asked me if I knew the person who was riding the animal, then a few rods in advance of us. I answered in the negative. 'Where does he say he is going?' enquired my friend. I told him that he said he was going to Ohio. 'He is not going to Ohio,' continued my friend; 'beware of him, for he is a suspicious fellow, who has been loitering around here for several weeks, for no good, I fear.' I told him that I had been sounding him for the last half hour, and had come to the conclusion, from the account he gave of himself, that he was not altogether right. He was either very fond of gasconade, or was a villain. My friend then cautioned me again to beware of him—that he thought he had some design upon me, or upon my horse and buggy—that likely he would follow me into the wilderness, and there attack me, assisted by confederates, who, perhaps, were to meet him in the Black swamp, a desolate region lying between Kirklin and the village of Boxley, on the Strawtown road. I told my friend that I had no weapons. He advised me to get a pistol, or knife, or both, before I attempted to cross the wilderness; and that, if he were in my place, under the circumstances, he would change the route, and take the Michigan road through Indianapolis, rather than go through the wilderness alone, or in company with this stranger. After my friend left us, the man on horseback related his horse-racing exploits in Missouri. He said the mare he was riding was a singe cat. That within the three previous years he had won large sums of money by running her against some of the swiftest race nags of Missouri and Illinois. I told him I had no doubt but that she was swift, but that I thought my old buggy horse, Proctor, could beat her on a race of one mile; and if he was willing, we would stop right there in the prairie, and I would take him out of the harness and run him against his mare one mile, and whoever won the race was to have both animals. I made this banter merely to bluff him, and check his vaunting, which it did in short order. On arriving at Wynkoop's tavern in Kirklin, I stopped awhile, in order to avoid the company of my fellow traveler, but he also stopped, and appeared determined to stick with me. I told Mr. Wynkoop, privately, that I did not fancy the company of my new acquaintance—that I had been cautioned to beware of him, and would be glad to purchase, or borrow, a pair of pistols to protect myself in case he should attack me on the way. Mr. W. had no weapons that would suit my purpose.

The stranger said the wilderness route by Strawtown was much nearer, and a better road, than we would have if we went round by Indianapolis. I knew it to be the nearest and best route to where I was going, besides I had business near Strawtown that called me that way, but I did not like my company. The thought of being driven out of my course by that impudent fellow, annoyed me very much. I finally concluded to run the risk of danger on the wilderness road, thinking that in a rough-and-tumble combat, if any such thing should happen, I would be a full match for my fellow traveler. We had not got three miles in the wilderness before there was a marked change in the demeanor of the horseman, whose bearing became more insolent and imperious. It was evident that he intended mischief. I detected him casting glances at the horse and buggy, and then at me, as if in doubt in what manner to make an attack. He occasionally checked up his horse and reined it over towards the side of the road occupied by me. I told him to trot ahead, and I would keep up with him. He would trot along for a few rods briskly, but soon showed a disposition to lag back, and try again to get behind me, which I was determined he should not do, if I could prevent it. After my speaking several times earnestly and rather sharply, for him to keep ahead, he at length dashed off some distance along the road, evincing by his manner that he was in an ill humor. I saw him take something from the breast pocket of his coat, the shadow of which upon the ground resembled a pistol, upon which I saw him, as I thought, put a percussion cap. He placed it back in his pocket, and drew out another instrument of some kind, which he examined and then placed back again. He soon fell behind me, in spite of all my remonstrances. I dashed ahead of him in a brisk trot, watching him as I passed. After stopping until I had got some hundred yards in advance of him, he raised himself in his stirrups, adjusted his coat skirts around him, then clenching the reins and mane firmly with his left hand, he came dashing up behind me at full gallop. I checked up my horse suddenly and turned round, facing him, at the same time I unwound the blanket from around the horn of my Spanish saddle, which I intended to grasp and hold up before me as a shield to ward off his bullets in case he fired at me. His eye caught sight of the black crooked horn or knob of my saddle, as it protruded above the blanket, which he took for the butt of a horseman's pistol, and instantly dashed off on the opposite side of the road, and sped by me at full speed, looking as black in the face as a thunder cloud. I saw the magical effect of the saddle knob, and hurriedly covered it over with the blanket, to keep up the impression that I had a pair of horseman's pistols wrapped in the blanket. From that time his ferocity seemed to abate, and he was more docile and civil in his language and manners. When we arrived at the town of Boxley, I stopped for dinner, and invited him to stop, but he declined, saying that he would press on, as he was anxious to get beyond Strawtown that night. I did not insist, and he passed on. On resuming my journey, I was on the look out, lest my forenoon companion might be secreted behind some large tree near the road, and might fire upon me from ambush. I enquired of the travelers and movers whom I met, if they had seen a man answering the description of him, who I described minutely. I found that he had passed along the road for about three or four miles east of Boxley, and then turned out into the woods. I continued to enquire for him until I reached White river, but never afterwards heard of him. I do not know, nor pretend to say, whether he really had any intention to try to rob me in the Black swamp, or whether he acted as he did to increase my fears, which I doubt not he plainly perceived. Be that as it may, I think in the end he was full as fearful of me as I was of him, and he was willing to quit, and call it a draw game.

CHAPTER XIV.

I regret that a want of space compels me to abandon my
original plan, which was to continue on with a list of the old
settlers of Boone, Carroll, White, Cass, Miami and other counties
of the upper Wabash, to do which I find would far exceed the
limits of this little volume. I shall, however, notice incidents
connected with the early settlement of these counties, as well as
others situated near them. Having had but little personal
acquaintance with what might be termed the lower Wabash
country, lying south of Vermillion and Parke counties, it could
not be expected that I would have many "Recollections" of that
beautiful, fertile and prosperous portion of the Wabash valley.

The natural scenery of the Wabash valley, as it was found by
the first settlers, although not bluffy and broken, was nevertheless
beautiful and picturesque. Hills and dales, forests and prairies,
grottos, rivulets and rivers, checkered and diversified every portion
of it.

It was in the month of April when I first saw the Wabash
river. Its green banks were lined with the richest verdure.
Wild flowers intermingled with the tall grass that nodded in
the passing breeze. Nature seemed clothed in her bridal robe.
Blossoms of the wild plum, hawthorn and red-bud made the air
redolent. The notes of the black-bird and blue-jay mingled with
the shrill cry of the king-fisher, river-gull and speckled loon.
On the points of the islands, cranes and herons were carrying on

piscatorial adventures among the unwary minnies that had ventured into the coves that indented the islands. Large flocks of wild geese, brants, and ducks, occasionally passed over head, or would light down into the bayous and hold a general carnival. It was rare sport for the young Nimrods of the neighborhood to fix up their "blinds" around those duck ponds, and "bag" more game than they could carry home at a load. Schools of fishes—salmon, bass, red-horse, and pike—swam close along the shore, catching at the blossoms of the red-bud and plum that floated on the surface of the water, which was so clear that myriads of the finny tribe could be seen darting hither and thither amidst the limpid element, turning up their silvery sides as they sped out into deeper water.

Perhaps no country ever produced a greater variety of wild fruits and berries. The wide fertile bottom lands of the Wabash, in many places presented one continuous orchard of wild plum and crab-apple bushes, overspread with arbors of the different varieties of the woods grape, wild hops, and honeysuckle fantastically wreathed together. One bush, or cluster of bushes, often presenting the crimson plum, the yellow crab-apple, the blue luscious grape, festoons of matured wild hops, mingled with the red berries of the clambering sweet-briar, that bound them all lovingly together. Gooseberries and strawberries were the first gathered by the early settlers. They were soon succeeded by blackberries, dewberries and raspberries, which grew thickly in the fence corners, in the woods, and in the vicinity of clearings and fallen timber. In more sterile, sandy regions were to be found the huckleberry, whortleberry, and in wet and marshy districts cranberries grew in great abundance. The cranberry marshes, in many portions of northwestern Indiana, are of great value—furnishing vast amounts of berries, which are gathered at the proper season and shipped to the various markets for hundreds of miles around. Pond Grove, in Tippecanoe county, is a valuable property to its owner, furnishing large crops of this excellent berry, which is a staple article in the culinary calendar of the best hotels and private families.

Black walnuts, butter nuts, hickory and hazel nuts grew in great profusion throughout the Wabash country. A few persimmon bushes and apple trees, planted no doubt by the French and Indians, were found growing near the old Indian town on the north side of the Wea prairie, above the mouth of Indian creek. Between Terre Haute and Vincennes, and between the latter place and the mouth of the Wabash, pecan and chestnut trees in many places were quite common. These nuts were gathered and hulled by the juveniles in the Fall, and cracked around the cabin hearth during the long Winter nights, while the father and mother rehearsed to their listening children the stirring incidents that transpired during their childhood on the Monongahela, Scioto, or in old Kentuck.

Were I to stop here, after describing the "deep tangled wild-wood," diversified with hills and dales, brooks and rivers, and the delicious wild fruits and berries that everywhere grew in our picturesque and fertile Wabash valley, and in the language of America's great poet, were to allude to the

> Gardens of the desert,
> The unshorn fields, boundless and beautiful—
> For which the speech of England has no name—

the prairies—and were then to leave them mantled in the verdure and sunlight that originally invested them, my work would be unfinished.

The gofer and the prairie-hawk, the wolf and the rattlesnake, with the many other drawbacks that surrounded and annoyed our early settlers, should be adverted to.

Black, grey and prairie wolves were quite numerous, and in many localities it was next to impossible to raise sheep or pigs until they had been hunted out. The Legislature enacted laws granting a bounty on wolf scalps, sufficient to stimulate a more active and thorough extermination of these noisy serenaders, who would often approach within a few rods of the cabin, and make night hideous with their prolonged howling. Wolf hunts were then common, in which the inhabitants of several neighborhoods, and sometimes of a whole county, took part. They were usually conducted in the following manner: The territory to be hunted over was circumscribed by four lines, sufficiently distant from each other to enclose the proper area. To each line was assigned a captain, with his subaltern officers, whose duty it was to properly station his men along the line, and at the hour agreed upon to cause them to advance in order towards the centre of the arena. The lines all charged simultaneously towards the centre, on horseback, with dogs, guns and clubs, thus completely investing whatever game was within the lines, and scaring it from the advancing lines toward the centre, where the excitement of the chase was greatly heightened, and the greatest carnage ensued. Often from two to ten wolves and as many deer were taken in a day at these hunts, and wild cats, foxes and catamounts in abundance. Horses and dogs soon became fond of the sport, and seemed to enter into it with a zest surpassing that of their masters. Solomon Slayback lost a fine horse in a wolf hunt, near Pond Grove, in early times. McDonald's celebrated charger, Selim, that bore his gallant master in many a charge against the British cavalry, in the Revolutionary war, was scarcely a more noble animal. Sol's horse went thundering along a few rods in the rear of a prairie wolf, and a full half mile ahead of every other horseman, when he plunged one of his fore legs into a wolf hole, which was partially concealed in the grass, turned a summerset, snapped his leg below the knee, and threw his rider several rods in the grass. The wolf escaped. Slayback escaped without any serious bodily harm, but the noble horse's leg was so badly fractured that recovery was deemed impossible, and he was killed to put him out of his misery.

There was another subtle and dangerous enemy to the early inhabitants, that legislative enactments could not reach, and the most cautious vigilance of the settler could not guard against. The "snake in the grass," in all its fearful varieties, were not only common, but exceedingly numerous in the country. Besides the rattlesnake, viper, adder, and blood-snake, there were a great many large blue and green snakes in the prairie districts, quite saucy and pugnacious, that delighted to give chase to new-comers, and frighten them by their hostile attitudes and convolutions. If you would retreat, they would chase you like a regular black racer; but if you would turn and give them battle, they would immediately retreat with all possible speed, glide off into the grass, and wait for a "greener customer" to pass along, when they would again dart out at him as if they were boa-constrictors, determined to take their prey. These snakes were harmless, but served to put people upon their guard for their more dangerous and venomous relatives, whose poisonous fangs were greatly dreaded by all.

William Robinson, Esq., during the early settlement on the Little Wea, was bitten by a rattlesnake, and although every remedy within reach of his friends was applied, he died of the wound. William Key, who lived in Wabash township, west of Lafayette, was also bitten by a rattlesnake, and was cured by the immediate and constant application of the usual antidote in such cases.

Many persons, in different sections of the country, beside a still larger number of cattle and horses, during every Summer, suffered from the poisonous fangs of these venomous reptiles, which infested every portion of the country. Early in the Spring, and late in the Fall, certain localities seemed to teem with these scaly monsters, while other places became comparatively free from them, which induced the belief that they took up their Winter quarters near those places where they assembled late in the Fall. Strict search was instituted, and in the Spring of 1827–28, two snake dens were discovered in the vicinity of Lafayette—one in a deep ravine about half a mile west of Lafayette, where the road ascends the hill going to Kingston, and the other on the north side of the Big Wea creek, near Bear's spring, about one-half mile northeast of Foresman's mill. As soon as it was certainly known that these dens existed beyond doubt, word was sent through the different neighborhoods for the citizens to meet at these dens on certain days mentioned in the notice, with mattocks, spades and crow-bars. If the clefts in the rocks were such that the snakes could be dug out, they went to work, and after breaking through their subterranean citadel, brought out scores of torpid rattlesnakes, and "bruised their heads" into a pummice, and left them to be devoured of hogs. Some of the fattest were taken home, and gallons of oil extracted from their carcasses; and their glittering skins carefully saved to cure rheumatism, and other chronic disorders, for which they were deemed a wonderful specific. If the digging process was found to be impracticable, stakes were driven in the ground close to each other, three or four feet high, enclosing a sufficient area around the hole to admit of a large egress of the reptile tribe beneath. One end of a long pole was placed on a line of picketing, while the other end of this horizontal shaft or lever formed a right angle with another short perpendicular shaft, the lower end of which was placed immediately over the hole in such a manner that, upon hoisting the other end of the lever, by pulling on a long grapevine attached to the end of the same, this sharpened perpendicular shaft was thrust into the hole, stopping it as completely as a cob would a jug.

After thus setting their trap, the snake-hunters left with the understanding that all hands were to meet at the den the next warm, sunny day, after the garter-snakes were first seen on the sunny side of the hills. At the time appointed the inhabitants for many miles around met at the selected place. If the weather had been sufficiently warm and balmy to draw out a large number of snakes to bask in the sun, the grapevine was pulled, the lever sprung, the hole stopped, and the snakes belabored with hoop poles and bludgeons prepared for the purpose, and thus hundreds were entrapped and killed in a day.

A few years of snake-killing in this wholesale manner, comparatively rid the country of these dangerous serpents; and it is only once in a great while that one of these large, black and yellow rattlesnakes are to be seen.

CHAPTER XV.

FIRST QUARTERLY MEETING OF THE METHODISTS AT LAFAYETTE— JOHN STRANGE AND JAMES ARMSTRONG—LITERARY SOCIETIES OF LAFAYETTE—LECTURES ON FLUNKEYISM—CAPTAIN PRICE'S CLASS IN MNEMONICS.

The first quarterly meeting of the Methodist Episcopal church held in Lafayette, met in a log cabin, long afterward used by Eli Huntsinger as a wheel wright shop, which stood on the corner of Mississippi and Ferry streets, within a few rods of the chapel of the Western Charge of the Methodist church.

James Armstrong was the circuit rider, and John Strange presiding elder. The district then embraced western Indiana, which extended from the Ohio river northward to the lakes, and the circuit was scarcely less extensive.

These able and beloved ministers of the gospel, with a self-sacrificing devotion to the spiritual interests of their flocks, made it a point never to fail meeting their congregations, however small in point of numbers, when it was possible to prevent it. The circuit rider had published the time and place of the quarterly meeting for more than a month, and many of the Methodist and other denominations scattered throughout the sparsely settled neighborhoods of the country, had assembled with the few church members who resided in Lafayette, to worship the Almighty, and cultivate and strengthen the bonds of social society. Besides public preaching, and the transaction of the business of the quarterly conference, a Love Feast was held, according to the usages of the society, and the Lord's Supper was administered in a solemn and appropriate manner.

Armstrong, who was an eloquent and popular preacher, beloved by all who knew him, addressed the meeting with happy effect; and Strange, a man of surpassing personal beauty, piety and eloquence, conducted the services of the Eucharist.

While Strange was addressing the communicants bowed around the altar, and in the most soothing and encouraging language pointed them to Christ as the "Lamb of God that taketh away the sins of the world," a group of giddy, thoughtless young men sat near the door, whose looks and actions denoted a spirit of levity wholly incompatible with the solemn ceremonies transpiring before them. Strange for awhile seemed to take no notice of their whispering, and throwing hazel nut hulls over the floor, but continued to address the communicants in the most gentle and touching manner; and then he started up suddenly, as if awaking from a reverie, and said: "Did I say Christ was the Lamb of God? —he is, to the humble, penitent believer; but to you," (pointing back with his long, bony finger toward the young men near the door,) "to you, sinner, arouse him, and he is the Lion of the tribe of Judea; and by the slightest exertion of his omnific finger, could dash you deeper into damnation than a sunbeam could fly in a million of ages!" The effect was electrical. The transition from the gentle and pathetic to the stern and terrible, was so sudden and unexpected, that one of the young men said he felt his hair instantly raise on end, and that he was going with the velocity of thought toward the doleful regions so eloquently and

6

fearfully alluded to in this impromptu and brilliant flash of rhetoric, which equalled the most sublime flights of Bridaine, Bascom, or Simpson.

Armstrong, Strange, and the most of those who were present at that quarterly meeting, have passed to that "bourne from whence no traveler returns." A few only of those who partook of the Eucharist on that occasion linger among us. The young gentleman who was the leader of the disturbers near the door that evening, and felt that he was flying through space to Pandemonium swifter than Milton's "Arch Angel Ruined" ever did, still lives in Lafayette, and is now a worthy and exemplary member of church. When I see his grey head, as he moves around town, with his hair standing *a la* Jackson, I secretly wonder whether it is natural for his hair to resemble the "fretful porcupine," or whether it was not caused by the electric shock of Strange's potent eloquence

It was my design originally to have given a somewhat lengthy notice of the organization and progress of the various churches and schools, as well as the several literary societies that from time to time flourished in Lafayette—beginning as far back as the debating society held in the old court ho se, which was organized and attended by O. L. Clark, Joseph Tatman, Albert S. White, Wm. M. Jenners, John Pettit, Thomas B. Brown, John B. Semans, Samuel A. Huff, David Jennings, John D. Farmer, Ezekiel Timmons, Cyrus Ball, David Ross, John Taylor, William F. Reynolds, N. H. Stockwell, Sandford C. Cox, John D. Smith, Dr. Jackson, and various others, whose names will appear by reference to the archives of the venerable institution.

But a mere glance at the many interesting incidents that might be adverted to, admonishes me that such a course would lead me beyond the restricted limits of these pages. I must content myself with a brief allusion to the several literary societies and clubs that successively flourished in Lafayette.

Mr. Town's grammar school succeeded the debating club above alluded to, and at its close the Tippecanoe county lyceum was inaugurated, which was largely attended by the *literati*, male and female, of the village and surrounding country, and was a pleasant and profitable institution for several years. But pork, grain and beef, and commerce generally, got the upper hand of literature, and the lyceum, which had many members and honorary members possessing the finest order of talents, who have since filled high and honorable stations in the various departments of life, was suffered to languish and expire.

The lyceum was succeeded by the "Hard Knot," a literary association composed of the most ardent and devoted members of the former societies, who were determined that a Philomathean spirit should not entirely die out in our town. During the hum and bustle of commerce, while our little city was the focal point of a circle of trade that extended for fifty or one hundred miles around, this little society worked as a leven, preparing community for the Franklin Club, which flourished several years, and appeared for awhile as the Phœnix which sprung from the ashes of the old lyceum. In a few years the majority of the members of this popular society relapsed into their former commercial habits, and grain, pork, canals, railroads, and banks and banking were the all-absorbing topics. Only a few real mourners followed the corpse of this society to its grave.

About this time, with the expanding fortunes of some worthy citizens of our growing town, there appeared to be mixed a slight leven of aristocracy, which some feared might in time, if not checked, create heart-burnings and jealousies in the community, by establishing castes and grades in social life, based more upon wealth than merit.

Innovation, though in silver slippers, excited not only the distrust, but the marked opposition, of a majority of our citizens, and among them many of the most able and influential inhabitants of the place. A course of lectures on *Flunkeyism*, delivered to large and admiring audiences, by one who knew how to deal in the most scalding sarcasm, completely cured the growing distemper, and it is now thought by good judges that our community has never since been afflicted with the slightest symptoms of that bogus aristocracy, which is prone to steal into pantalette towns, villages, and even rural districts, if not carefully guarded against, and nipped in the bud.

These lectures were succeeded by the Moot Legislature of Lafayette, a large and interesting body, which numbered over one hundred members, and was conducted with an ability that would not have been discreditable to the real Legislature of the State for two or three consecutive Winters.

While in this connection it would be proper to allude to Capt. Price's class in Mnemonics, or the art of memory, in which he proposed in a course of eight lectures, to learn his pupils to memorise and repeat fifty or more of the hardest words that could be propounded, by simply naming them over once. He assured them, also, that they would be able to repeat them in their exact order, from the first to the fiftieth; and then pass over them backwards from No. 50 to No. 1, without miscalling a word in their regular order. The Captain further assured his class, that he would not only teach them to recollect and recall backward and forward in its numerical order, but also to answer correctly the word at every number as soon as the number was called for.

He succeeded beyond all expectations, and on the fourth evening had learned his class so that the dullest member could repeat over one hundred of the hardest words, by the power of association. The whole class graduated simultaneously, and dismissed the learned professor with a vote of thanks, and a written certificate of his marvelous powers as a teacher of the science of mnemonics.

Upon the demise of the Franklin Club, a new society sprung up, in which there was a spirited contest as to what name it should have. Many and various were the names proposed, all quite classic and significant, any of which would have been appropriate enough, but so fastidious were its members in regard to the name, and each one was so prepossessed in favor of the particular cognomen proposed by himself, that like many a darling infant, it went a long time before a name good enough for it could be found and adopted. At length, after a month of weekly and semi-weekly meetings of the society, at all of which the name was the great cardinal point discussed, some astute member hit upon the word *Hocofelto*. It had a classic jingle in it, and struck the ears of a majority favorably. It was voted upon and adopted as the name of the Club.

After while some of the members desired to know the meaning of the word Hocofelto, and hinted that it might be proper for a band of Philomatheans to be able to explain the meaning of the term used to designate the name of their society, even were it dug up from the learned rubbish of a defunct literature. The member who proposed the name was called upon for a definition of the word. He declined giving it. Lexicons and Donnegons were carefully examined by experts in the learned languages, but no clue could be got to the etymology of the extraordinary word that had been adopted as the name of the society. The most erudite of the society felt deeply chagrined that this name had been adopted with such imprudent haste, before its signification, if it had any, had been ascertained. Had the society been dubbed Hifalutin, Ompompanoosuc, or any such high-sounding term, that would have had some specific meaning, they could have borne it better. But as the society had been progressing publicly for several weeks under this truly abstruse name, it was thought best not to change it; that the enigma of the name would secure the profound admiration of a gaping world, who, as some ill-natured philosophers have intimated, are prone to admire and venerate that which is above their comprehension. So every member redoubled his efforts to carry out the laudable objects for which the society had been organized, and add another proof to the world that "the rose would smell as sweet by any other name." All acted upon the wise suggestion, and though, on the subject of the name, they were as grave and sombre as a squad of Sons of Malta, the Hocofelto Club flourished for many years, and was excelled in usefulness and longevity by none of its predecessors, with the single exception of the Hard Knot, which will ever remain enshrined in the memories of its members as long as the vital current courses through their veins.

CHAPTER XVI.

BLACK HAWK WAR—SAC VILLAGE AT THE MOUTH OF ROCK RIVER—
FORT ARMSTRONG—BLACK HAWK'S TOWER—FIRST BATTLE—
TROOPS MARCH FROM LAFAYETTE AND OTHER POINTS.

In the Spring of 1832, the renowned Sac Chief, Black Hawk, and his followers, were unwilling to leave the lands on the eastern bank of the Mississippi, which had been ceded to the United States by treaty with the Sacs and Foxes—held at Prairie du Chien in July, 1830.

Black Hawk's headquarters were at the Sac village, at the mouth of Rock river, almost within cannon shot of Fort Armstrong, on Rock Island, where General Atkinson was then stationed with several companies of United States troops.

A short distance above the mouth of Rock river may yet be seen the celebrated point or eminence known as "Black Hawk's Tower," a bald and lofty peak of the Rock river hills, near the bridge on the road leading from Camden to Rock Island. From the top of a tree that stood upon the apex of this peak, the old Sachem and his spies were wont to overlook the Mississippi and Rock rivers, and their valleys, for many miles distant, from whence they could descry the approach of an enemy by land or water, long before they could obtain a dangerous proximity.

General Atkinson at first expostulated with the Indians—told them that their rashness would result in great injury to themselves—that the United States had purchased the lands by a fair treaty, and would maintain their title at every hazard; and that it would be folly in the extreme for Black Hawk and his malcontents to attempt to oppose our government troops, which were as numerous as the leaves of the forest. The implacable old Chief turned a deaf ear to every kind overture, and was determined to take up the tomahawk to maintain the possession of the home of his childhood, and the soil that contained the graves of his ancestors.

Dreading the blow that Gen. Atkinson meditated giving him with his regulars, and a few companies of militia which had been hastily called together, Black Hawk withdrew up the Rock river, with his forces, passing through the Winnebago swamps, causing great alarm among the frontier settlers.

Governor Reynolds, of Illinois, issued a stirring call to the people of his State to take up arms, which was responded to by large companies of volunteer militia, from various portions of the State. On the 14th of May, a detachment of over two hundred men, commanded by Major Stillman, attacked an inferior number of Indians on Sycamore creek, about thirty miles from Dixon's Ferry on Rock river, but were compelled to retire with considerable loss. This was the first action in the Black Hawk war. On the day following, General Whitesides, who was then at Dixon's Ferry, hastened to the scene of action with a force of fifteen hundred men, but was unable to find the enemy.

The commanding officer at Fort Dearborn, or Chicago, gave intelligence that fifteen persons had been murdered on Hickory creek, and that the hostile Indians were assembling within forty miles of Chicago. The news flew rapidly in every direction.

On Sunday morning, the 18th of May, 1832, the people on the west side of the Wabash river, were thrown into a state of great consternation on account of a report reaching them that a large body of hostile Indians had approached within fifteen miles of Lafayette, and killed two men. The alarm soon spread throughout Tippecanoe, Warren, Vermillion, Fountain, Montgomery, and adjoining counties. Several brave commandants of companies on the west side of the Wabash, in Tippecanoe county, raised troops to go and meet the enemy, and dispatched an express to General Walker, with a request that he should make a call upon the militia of the county, to equip themselves *instanter*, and march to the aid of their bleeding countrymen. Thereupon Gen. Walker, Col. Davis, Lt. Col. Jenners, Capt. Brown, of the *artillery*, and various other gallant spirits, mounted their war steeds and proceeded to the *army*, and from thence upon a scout into the Grand prairie, to discover, if possible, the number, situation, and intention of the Indians.

Old men, women and children, to the number of over three hundred, flocked precipitately to Lafayette and the surrounding country, on the east side of the Wabash river. An incident occurred during the general stampede that deserves to be recorded:

A Mr. D——, who, with his wife and seven children, resided on the edge of the Grand prairie, west of Lafayette, in a locality considered as particularly dangerous, made hurried preparations to fly with his family to Lafayette for safety. Imagine his surprise and chagrin, when his "better half" told him that she would not go one step—that she did not believe in being scared at trifles, and that in her opinion there was not an Indian within one hundred miles. Importunity proved unavailing, and the disconsolate and scared husband and father gathered up all the children except the babe, and bid his wife and infant child a long and solemn adieu, never expecting to see them again, unless perhaps he might find their mangled remains, minus their scalps. On arriving at Lafayette, his acquaintances rallied and berated him for abandoning his wife and child in the hour of peril; but he met their jibes with a stoical indifference, averring that he should not be held accountable for her obstinacy. As the shades of evening drew on, Mrs. D. felt lonely, and the chirping of the frogs and notes of the whippoorwill increased her loneliness, until she halfway wished she had accompanied the rest of the family in their flight. After staying a few hours in the house without striking a light, she concluded that perhaps the old adage, "discretion is the better part of valor," was true, she arose, took some bed clothes off of one of the beds, passed out, fastened the cabin door, and hastened with her babe on her bosom to a sink-hole in the woods, some few hundred yards from the house, in which she said that she and her babe in the woods slept soundly until sunrise the next morning.

The little town of Lafayette literally boiled over with people and patriotism. A public meeting was held at the court house. Speeches were made by sundry patriotic individuals, and, to allay the fears of the women, an armed police was immediately voted, to be called the Lafayette Guards. An organization took place immediately. Thomas T. Benbridge was elected captain, and

John Cox lieutenant. Captain Benbridge yielded the active drill of the Guards to his lieutenant, who had served two years in the war of 1812. After the meeting at the court house adjourned, the Guards were paraded on the green where Purdue's block now stands, and put through sundry military evolutions, by Lieut. Cox, who proved to be an expert drill officer, whose clear, shrill voice rung out on the night air; as he marched and countermarched the troops from where the paper mill stands to Main street ferry, and over the suburbs generally. Every old gun and sword that could be found were brought into requisition, with a new shine on them.

Gen. Walker, Cols. Davis and Jenners, and other commissioned and non-commissioned officers, joined in a call on the people of Tippecanoe county, for volunteers to march to the protection of the frontier settlers. A large meeting of the citizens assembled on the public square in Lafayette, and over three hundred volunteers, mostly mounted men, left Lafayette for the purpose of repairing to the point of danger, with an alacrity that would have done credit to veterans.

They camped the first night about nine miles west of Lafayette, near the edge of the Grand prairie. After placing out sentinels for the night, the troops retired to rest. A few of the subaltern officers, without consulting with their superiors, very injudiciously concluded to try what effect a *false alarm* would have upon the sleeping soldiers, and a few of them, with others initiated into the important secret, withdrew to a neighboring thicket, and from thence made a charge on the picket guards, who, after hailing them and receiving no countersign, fired off their guns, and run for the Colonel's marquee in the centre of the encampment. The aroused Colonels and their staff, who had been kept in ignorance of the *ruse*, sprung to their feet, shouting "to arms!" "to arms!" and the obedient and panic-stricken soldiers seized their guns, and demanded to be led against the invading foe. A wild scene of disorder ensued. Amid the din of arms, firing of guns, and loud commands of officers, the raw militia felt that they had already got into the red jaws of battle. One of the alarmed sentinels, in running to the centre of the encampment, leaped over a blazing camp fire, and lit full upon the breast and stomach of a sleeping counsellor of the law, who was no doubt at that moment dreaming of vested and contingent remainders, rich clients and good fees—which, in legal parlance was suddenly *estopped* by the hob-nails in the stogas of the scared sentinel. As soon as the counsellor's vitality and consciousness sufficiently returned, he put in some strong demurrers to the conduct of the affrighted picket-man, averring that he would greatly prefer being wounded by the enemy, to being run over by a cowardly booby.

Next morning the officer in command administered a salutary reprimand to the getters-up of the false alarm of the previous night—showing the glaring impropriety of such conduct, and the bad consequences that might have resulted from such insubordination and unmilitary conduct, and gave them plainly to understand that if they or others attempted the like again, they might expect the most rigorous penalty of a court martial.

Monday morning an express was received from his Excellency Governor Noble, of Indiana, to Brigadier General Jacob Walker, approving the measures adopted by our officers, for the safety and repose of our frontiers, and directing him to call out his whole command, if necessary, and supply our men with arms, horses, and provisions, procuring them by seizure or otherwise. On the next day four baggage wagons were dispatched, loaded with camp equipages, and such stores, provisions, and other articles as were necessary for the comfort and convenience of our fellow citizens in arms, who were amply provided for a tour of five or six weeks.

Thursday, May 31st, a fine looking squad of mounted men from Putnam county, Indiana, commanded by Col. Sigler, passed through Lafayette, for the hostile region; and on the 13th of June, Col. A. W. Russell, commandant of the 40th regiment of Indiana militia, passed through Lafayette with 340 mounted volunteers, from the counties of Marion, Hendricks, and Johnson, on their way to the scene of hostilities. Several companies of volunteers from Montgomery, Fountain and Warren counties, hastened to the relief of the frontier settlers of Indiana and Illinois. The troops from Lafayette, after marching to Sugar creek, and remaining there a few days without finding an enemy, or any very strong probability of finding any east of the O'Plein river, were ordered to return by Gen. Walker.

The troops all acquiesced, except about forty-five horsemen, who filed off, and said they would form an independent company

of volunteers, and would proceed beyond Hickory creek, where
the depredations had been committed by the Indians. The company was organized by electing Samuel McGeorge, a soldier of
the war of 1812, captain, and Amos Allen and Andrew W.
Ingraham lieutenants.

CHAPTER XVII.

CAPTAIN M'GEORGE MARCHES TO THE O'PLEIN—ISRAEL H. COX WOUND-
ED—RETURN OF M'GEORGE'S COMPANY—GENERAL SCOTT AND HIS
TROOPS ARRIVE AT CHICAGO—CHOLERA AMONG THE TROOPS—
BATTLE OF THE BLUE MOUNDS—BLACK HAWK DEFEATED ON THE
BANK OF THE MISSISSIPPI—HIS CAPTIVITY AND DEATH.

In a few hours after their organization, Captain McGeorge's
company proceeded on their march toward Hickory creek, determined to partake of the dangers and glory of the war. They
pressed beyond Hickory creek, as far as the O'Plein river, without meeting with any of the hostile Indians. Finding no enemy
to encounter, they concluded to return. On the first night, as
they returned, they encamped on the open prairie, near a grove
on Hickory creek, and placed out sentinels as usual. The night
was dark and cloudy, and it began to rain about ten o'clock,
rendering it difficult for the sentinels to keep their guns dry.
Captain Israel H. Cox, and a man by the name of Fox, were
placed within fifteen or twenty paces of each other as sentinels,
by the sergeant of the guard. Cox wore a shingle-cape overcoat,
a skirt of which he drew over his gun lock to keep it dry, which
motion Fox perceived, and, taking him for an Indian, fired upon
him, the ball passing through the belt of his overcoat, striking
the brass hilt of a dagger which the Captain wore by his side,
and then glancing downward through the thigh, fracturing the
bone. After a moment's pause, several soldiers ran toward the
place where the flash of the gun had been seen; but a voice,
"Don't shoot him—it was a sentinel who shot me!" caused them

to lower their guns, which were cocked and leveled on the individual who fired the gun. They hurried to the prostrate man, whose wound was bleeding profusely, which was soon dressed by the surgeon of the company.

Next morning the surgeon pronounced it improper to attempt to take the wounded man along with the company. So he was left behind in care of his two brothers, Joseph and James Cox, David Marsh and Joseph Crouch, who, after his wound would permit, removed him in a litter to Col. Moore's company of Illinois militia, then encamped on the O'Plein, where the town of Joliet now stands, where he remained under the treatment of the surgeon of the Illinois troops, until he was able to be hauled home in a wagon, which his friends caused to be sent for him. It was several months before he was able to walk without crutches, and never entirely recovered from the lameness occasioned by the wound.

While on the subject of accidents which occurred during this war, it may not be improper to name two other sad mishaps, that cast a gloom over the feelings of their companions in arms. While a company of volunteers were passing through Fountain county, on their way to the point of danger, a squad of the rank and file discovered a large rattlesnake near the roadside, which they forthwith attacked, and just as one of the party pulled trigger to shoot the snake through the head, another of the company unluckily sprung across before the muzzle of the gun, receiving the rifle ball that was intended for the snake in his ankle, fracturing it badly.

The other occurred thus: On the night of the return of our troops from Sugar creek, Illinois, while Major Milhollen was marching the troops around the public square of Lafayette to muster them out of service, he commanded them to fire off their guns in platoons, in doing which one of the soldier's guns went off accidentally, and the paper wad struck Jonathan Tanner, one of the volunteers, in the side, producing a deep and dangerous wound, which for a long time threatened his life, but from which he subsequently recovered, after long confinement and much suffering.

Although the main body of the troops from Lafayette returned within eight or nine days, yet the alarm among the people was such that they could not be induced for some time to return to their farms, which greatly needed their attention.

Captain Newell, of Warren county, and twenty-five scouts, pressed out as far as Hickory creek, and beyond, and finding no enemy, returned just about the time the troops were leaving Lafayette. They met Mr. Hazzleton, of Fox river, and Mr. Reed, of O'Plein river, who reported that a party of the Illinois militia had been engaged with the Sacs at Rock Island, and had been defeated; and that the Indian agent at Chicago deemed it advisable for the people on Hickory creek to retreat to some place of safety; which information Capt. Newell communicated by letter addressed to John McCormick, of Lafayette, dated May 23, 1832, which letter was published in the Lafayette Free-Press, at that time printed and published by Major John B. Semans, an able and truthful journalist, who published the pioneer newspaper of the upper Wabash, and who enjoyed during his long and prosperous career in public life, the respect and confidence of all who knew him. He was a kind and affectionate husband and father, a true friend, and on his death-bed exemplified the appropriateness of the words of the poet:

> The chamber where the good man meets his fate,
> Is privileged beyond the common walks of life,
> Quite in the verge of Heaven.

The writer is under many obligations to Messrs. Luse & Wilson, editors and publishers of the Lafayette Daily Journal, for access to old files of the Free-Press, the oldest newspaper printed in western Indiana, from which their weekly and Daily Journal has descended in a direct line—the weekly having been a regular and continuous newspaper for more than thirty years past. He also acknowledges that he has obtained much valuable data by reference to the pages of the Western Annals, and manuscript letters, and other memoranda, furnished by friends.

The frontier settlements of Indiana, from Vincennes to Laporte, were rife with war news, and the people were upon the look-out for the invading foe, whose presence was hourly expected by the masses. Even our friends in Clinton county gathered into forts, and prepared for a regular siege; while our neighbors at Crawfordsville had their equanimity disturbed, by the arrival of a courier who entered the town at full speed, with the startling intelligence that the Indian forces, more than a thousand strong, were then actually crossing the Nine Mile prairie, about twelve miles north of town, killing and scalping all before them. Immediately precautionary measures were taken to protect the inhabitants, who were hurriedly gathered into the strongest houses, around which sentinels were placed, as well as at the mouths of the streets, ravines, and fords of the river, in the direction of the enemy. Scouts were sent out under the command of the bravest and most experienced woodsmen, to reconnoitre, and watch the movements of the advancing foe, while others were detailed in different directions through the country, to inform the population of the rural districts of impending danger, and urging them to hasten with their families into town, to assist their fellow citizens in combating the hostile savages, whose whoops they momentarily expected to hear echoing through the dense woods, lying north of Sugar river. Evening came, but no Indians. At nightfall the scouts returned with the news that the Indians had not crossed the Wabash, but were hourly expected at Lafayette, which was reported to be in a state of siege. The citizens of Warren, Fountain, and Vermillion counties were alike terrified by the most exaggerated stories of Indian massacres, and assembled in blockhouses to protect themselves against the hostile bands of invaders, which were carrying dismay and desolation throughout the country.

It turned out that these efforts at defence were unnecessary, as the Indians were not within one hundred miles of these temporary fortifications. But that circumstance by no means argued a want of courage on the part of those who used these precautionary measures. They did not know but that there was actual danger, and they wisely acted upon the principle that "caution is the parent of safety." They were familiar with danger, and the bloody tragedies enacted in the early settlement of Kentucky and Ohio, were fresh in their memories. There were but few families then residing in the west, who had not lost some of their near relatives by the hostile Indians.

A few there were, mostly old soldiers, who insisted that the reports of hostility were generally exaggerated, and that the storm of the war-cloud would spend its violence over northwestern Illinois, and would never extend as far east as the Wabash. The massacres of the frontier settlers in Kentucky, Ohio, and the early settlements in Indiana territory, were not forgotten, and the settlers were loathe to return to their farms, to peril the lives of themselves and families.

They required some reliable assurances that there was no danger, before they would assume so fearful a responsibility. To allay public excitement, Brigadier General Jacob Walker, of the 20th Brigade of Indiana Militia, published a report in the Lafayette Free-Press, in which he stated that "after continuing at the encampment at Sugar Tree Grove a sufficient time to ascertain the true situation of affairs, he considered it his duty to discharge a portion of the troops," which were marched back into Tippecanoe county by Major Milhollen, and honorably discharged by him on the public square in the city of Lafayette.

N. D. Grover, sub-Indian agent at Logansport, wrote a letter to the citizens of Lafayette, under date of the 31st of May, which was also published in the Free-Press, stating that the Pottawatomie and Miami Indians would not join the hostile Indians. On the first day of June, Samuel Hoover, John Taylor, John McCormick, John B. Semans, and six or seven other prominent citizens of Lafayette, published an address through the columns of the Free-Press, to the people of Tippecanoe and surrounding counties, that most of the troops from Lafayette had returned, and that there was no danger of the Indians in this locality, as the Miamis and Pottawatomies did not intend joining the hostile Indians, calling upon the people to become quiet and return to their homes without apprehension of danger. Thus assured, the people by degrees recovered from the panic and returned to their farms and crops, which greatly needed their attention.

Among Captain A——'s company of volunteers, from ———, was a man but little beloved by his Captain and fellow soldiers, who regarded him as a troublesome customer, and tried to dissuade him from going to war, but go he would, despite of objections and remonstrances from every quarter.

Troublesome from the outset, he became more disagreeable to his fellow soldiers every day. When the company had got some hundred miles into Illinois, the officers were at a loss to know how to dispose of this camp-pest, whom they feared would by his awkwardness or recklessness accidentally shoot some of his comrades. The captain made known his dilemma to an officer high in command, who said he could relieve him by sending the obnoxious individual as bearer of an "important despatch" to ————. The soldier was called up, and his Captain and the superior officer made him acquainted with the important service he had been selected to perform. That in consideration ·of the high estimate placed upon his capacity and fidelity, he had been chosen to carry an important express to the town of ————, which demanded that he should travel with all possible dispatch, day and night, until the important document was delivered to the person to whom it was directed. True to the trust reposed in him, the bearer of the express faithfully performed the laborious service, with all possible dispatch. Jaded and travel-worn, he handed over the important paper. The seal was broken, and it contained the following words:

"Give the bearer of these lines a good kicking, for he is a troublesome, disagreeable fellow—a pest and a nuisance to his Captain and fellow soldiers. Kick him or not, just as you please, but don't let him return to bother us here.   ———— ————."

While matters were going on thus in Indiana, the war still continued to progress in Illinois. Black Hawk and his warriors, surrounded by battalions of well disciplined troops that threatened to overwhelm him, attempted to escape to the west bank of the Mississippi.

On the 21st of May a party of about twenty hostile Indians attacked the Indian creek settlement in Lasalle county, Illinois, and killed fifteen persons, and took several young women prisoners, who in July following were returned to their friends through the efforts of the Winnebagos.

On the 22d of May a party of spies were attacked, and four of them slain, and other massacres of the frontier settlers followed. The militia, called out by Gov. Reynolds to the number of three thousand, rendezvoused in June, near Peru; and marched to Rock river, where they were joined by the United States troops, the whole to be under the command of Gen. Brady.

An additional force of six hundred mounted men was ordered out; and Gen. Winfield Scott, with nine companies of artillery, hastened from the seaboard, by way of the lakes, to Chicago, to take part against the Indians, but did not arrive in time to render any material aid—the western troops having well-nigh wound up the war before he arrived. His troops suffered much during their passage over the lakes, and while at Chicago, from the ravages of the Asiatic cholera—an enemy by far more dangerous and destructive than the hostile Indians they made haste to confront.

Between Rock river and Galena, Major Demont, with about one hundred and fifty militia, met and repulsed Black Hawk and his two hundred followers. This skirmish took place on the 24th of June. The army continued to move up Rock river in pursuit of Black Hawk, and overtook him on the 21st of July, near the Wisconsin river, in the neighborhood of the Blue Mounds, where a severe engagement took place between a party of troops, under the command of General Henry, and the savages. It has been said that in this battle the Indians had fifty-two killed, while the loss on the part of General Henry's men was one killed and eight wounded.

On the 28th of July, the main army crossed the Wisconsin river in pursuit of Black Hawk, who was retiring toward the Mississippi, and on the 2nd of August he was overtaken and defeated on the bank of the Mississippi, nearly opposite the upper Iowa, with a loss of one hundred and fifty men, while of the whites, it has been said that but eighteen fell. This was the last battle of the Black Hawk war. Considering his fortunes as desperate, the foiled Chief fled, but was seized by the Winnebagos, and in twenty-five days after the battle, he was delivered to the officers of the United States, at Prairie du Chien, and himself and family were sent as hostages to Fort Monroe, in the Chesapeake, where they remained in June, 1833.

Black Hawk, in his life, says that at the last battle, as also in the engagement with Major Stillman, his flag of truce was disregarded by our troops, and hostilities thrust upon the Indians while they were suing for peace. After his release from captivity, the Chief returned to his native wilds, where he died.　　7

CHAPTER XVIII.

FIRST LAWYERS OF LAFAYETTE—FOREIGN ATTORNEYS—FIRST PHYSI-
CIANS OF LAFAYETTE AND TIPPECANOE COUNTY—MINISTERS OF
THE GOSPEL OF THE VARIOUS CHRISTIAN DENOMINATIONS IN
LAFAYETTE.

The early Bar of Lafayette consisted of the following named
attorneys, viz: Joseph Tatman, Joseph Cox, Andrew Ingram,
David Patton, Moses Cox, Albert S. White, William M. Jen-
ners, Thomas B. Brown, Aaron Finch, and John Pettit, who were
all the resident attornies up to the October term of the Tippecanoe
Circuit Court for the year 1831. Rufus A. Lockwood moved to
Lafayette in the Summer of 1832. The foreign attorneys who
visited our Courts in those early times, were Thomas H. Blake,
J. B. Chapman, P. M. Curry, E. M. Huntington, J. Vanmetre,
C. Fletcher, P. H. Patterson, James Rariden, W. Quarrels, C. D.
Morris, D. Rogers, John Law, Septimus Smith, James Farring-
ton, Edward A. Hannegan, Caleb B. Smith, T. D. Beard, Thos.
J. Evans, David Wallace, J. Stetson, J. Angle, Jos. A. Wright,
Henry S. Lane, William P. Bryant, S. C. Willson, R. A. Chan-
dler and Burrel B. Taylor.

Many of these attorneys came from the most remote sections of
the State—riding those "extensive judicial circuits" alluded to in
a former chapter of this work. To show the energy, industry,
and perseverance of those pioneer attorneys, in the prosecution of
their chosen profession, I would state that John Law came from
Vincennes; Blake, Huntington and Farrington from Terre Haute;
Fletcher, Quarrels and Morris from Indianapolis; Rariden from
Richmond; Caleb B. Smith from Connersville; Chapman from
Laporte; Wright and Bryant from Rockville; Evans, Patterson,
Hannegan and Wallace from Covington; Chandler from Williams-
port; and Lane, Curry, Angle, and Willson from Crawfordsville.

From this exhibit the reader will perceive that our early lawyers considered the whole State as one vast circuit, which they traversed on horseback, sometimes alone, and sometimes in squads, as set forth in the "Reminiscences" of the Hon. O. H. Smith, long before the days of turnpikes, railroads, canals, or telegraphs. To witness a troop of those early attorneys entering a village as they traveled the circuit, themselves and their horses bespattered with mud, and their huge port-manteaus surmounted with overcoat and umbrella, they resembled the forlorn hope of a company of mounted rangers, entering upon some daring and almost hopeless charge, or a caravan emerging from the desert of Sahara, blackened with heat and covered with dust. But, young disciple of Blackstone, don't smile at the grotesque appearance of these early counsellors, who endured the hardships and privations of frontier life to consecrate the Temple of Justice, and lay the deep and firm foundation of that system of jurisprudence whereon rest all our civil, political and religious rights. With not a tithe of the advantages you possess, many of those men just named rose to an eminence in their profession, and to fill high and honorable stations in the judicial and legislative departments of the country. Their long rides on horseback, along blind paths and dimly defined roads, crossing unbridged streams, sleeping in the open air, as they frequently had to do, and leading colts and driving steers home, taken on fees, fully developed their physical and intellectual energies, and gave them a vigor and self-reliance possessed by but few of our more modern students, who have been in the habit of reclining on damask and plush, and passing from court to court on railroad cars, where the jolting is scarcely sufficient to aid the digestion of the sumptuous dinners, which are often taken with as keen a relish as ever they devoured Coke, Kent, or Chitty. To prove the truth of the position just assumed, that hardships and obstacles should be regarded as disciplinary means, calculated to develop and strengthen the latent powers of the self-made man, I will state, that from the list of attorneys above named, six were afterwards chosen to fill the bench, viz: Bryant, Pettit, Wallace, Huntington, Law, and Ingram; nine were elected Representatives in Congress, viz: White, Pettit, Hannegan, Blake, Rariden, Law, Lane, Wallace, and Smith— and three of them—Albert S. White, John Pettit, and Edward

A. Hannegan, were elected to the office of United States Senator. Joseph A. Wright served two terms as Governor of the State, and is now United States minister at the court of Berlin. David Wallace was also Governor one term, was elected to Congress, and was afterwards elected Judge of the Common Pleas Court of Marion county. Thomas H. Blake was commissioner of the General Land Office under President Tyler. E. M. Huntington has for many years been Judge of the District Court of the United States for the State of Indiana. John Pettit is the present able and popular Chief Justice of Kansas; and Henry S. Lane the Republican candidate for Governor of this State, who received the nomination by acclamation. When Rufus A. Lockwood first came to Lafayette he was quite young. He soon formed a law partnership with A. S. White. It was not long before the young barrister had an opportunity to display his dormant talents, which, like the sparks of the smitten steel, needed intellectual attrition to elicit them in all their sparkling brilliancy. The firm of White & Lockwood were engaged to defend John H. Frank, indicted for the murder of John Woods, which occurred in an affray growing out of a bet on an election. All looked to Mr. White, who was one of the ablest and most popular lawyers in the State, to take the lead in this important case, which involved the life of their client. But knowing the ability, tact and energy of his young partner, who, up to that time, had not been properly appreciated, he determined to give the young man a chance to make his debut before the public as an advocate. Throughout the protracted trial, which was prosecuted with marked ability Lockwood exhibited a research and depth of thought beyond the expectations of all who heard him. But his main speech in defense of the prisoner, which occupied two days in its delivery, exhibited his giant intellect in all its gigantic proportions, and at once raised him to the rank of one of the ablest advocates of this or any other country. The prisoner was acquitted. Lockwood's fortune was made. His speech in the case was published, and by many good judges has been pronounced equal to the best efforts of those more distinguished advocates, whose speeches have been published as models of forensic eloquence. For many years he carried on an extensive and lucrative practice at Lafayette, and in all the courts of Indiana. Soon after the discovery of gold in

California, he, with many other eminent attornies from this and other States, sought the newly discovered El Dorado, which promised a new theatre, where they might win golden laurels and nuggets at the same time. Lockwood soon secured a large and lucrative practice in the city of San Francisco. He was called upon to defend a prisoner, who rested under the ban of the self-constituted vigilance committee, who had wrested the administration of the law from the hands of the legally constituted authorities of the State, and were meting out life and death to the accused according to their caprice, or the hasty, ill-digested evidence produced before their clamorous court, which was selected from the heterogeneous mass of citizens who chanced to be present at the trial. Lockwood loudly denounced this wanton assumption of power on the part of the committee, and demanded a fair trial for the prisoner. The power and popularity of the committee were then in their zenith. They insolently demanded the prisoner of the sheriff, and threatened personal violence to Lockwood if he persisted in his demands for a legal trial of the prisoner. He hurled defiance at these "lawless, bloody inquisitors," as he termed them, and warned them, in return, that unless they ceased from their mobocratic murders, he would soon have them dangling on the limbs of trees, as high as ever they had swung the victims of their lawless violence. Judge Lynch's sheriffs, bailiffs and posse hovered round to grab this lone defender of the law and the right, but a sight of the revolver and bowie-knife which peeped from the belt that encircled his stalwart form, caused them to shrink back without executing their designs, and this legal Hercules, clad in the panoply of the law, single-handed, like Luther and Tell, withstood the brawling mob, and displayed a physical and moral courage that challenged the admiration of his most inveterate foes. Such lofty heroism presents a sublime spectacle, happily illustrated by Goldsmith's beautiful lines:

> Like some tall cliff that rears its towering form,
> Swells from the vale, and midway leaves the storm;
> Though round its breast the rolling clouds are spread,
> Eternal sunshine settles on its head."

From that hour the power and influence of the vigilance committee began to wane, and in a short time law and order resumed their sway in the Golden State. Lockwood's character for nerve and legal attainments spread far and wide, and he had his choice of sides in many important suits, which yielded him both money and professional character. After the discovery of gold in Australia, he left San Francisco, and sought that far-off modern Opher, in quest of adventure and the glittering metal. Soon after his arrival there, he was called on to make a Fourth of July oration, which he delivered with his wonted fervid eloquence, and produced quite a sensation among all who listened to it. Her Majesty's officers, some of whom listened to his speech, on looking over the map of the world, and seeing the immense distance Australia lay from the little island where Her Majesty's throne was situated, thought it not best to let such inflammatory speeches be made, fearing that a Cataline might be ensconced in the habiliments and character of a Yankee lawyer, which they called him, who might raise a rebellion that would wrest the auriferous island from the paw of the British Lion. Not wishing to excite a hub-bub among the loyal subjects of Her Imperial Majesty, he quietly retired from the crowded mart of Melbourne, to a rural retreat, where he hired to a farmer to attend a large flock of sheep, where in the character and employment of a shepherd, he "watched his flocks by night" and day, no doubt on the primitive plan, "leading them to green pastures, and by the side of still waters," for one year. After fulfilling his engagement as shepherd, he laid aside his crook, doffed his shepherd frock, and returned to San Francisco, where he resumed his practice of the law. He was employed by Col. John C. Fremont, in his great land suit for his Mariposa gold mine: He gained the case for Fremont, for which he was to receive a fee of one hundred thousand dollars. Soon after gaining this important suit, he embarked with his family to return to Lafayette, on board the ill-fated steamer Central America, which was wrecked on the ocean between Panama and New York, and the gifted and lamented Lockwood, with more than three hundred other passengers, found a watery grave. His wife and children were saved by the generous and magnanimous Captain Herndon, who preferred to perish himself with the wreck, rather than lose any of the women and children on board.

Next I will give a list of the early physicians of Lafayette, viz: Othniel L. Clark, J. N. Bradfield, James Davis, Robert Martin, Loyal Fairman, David Jennings, Nathan Jackson, Benj. Carlisle, Elizur Deming, I. N. Bladen, and Luther Jewett.[4] Of these, only three remain in the practice in this city, to-wit: Clark, Jennings, and Jewett. Bradfield, Bladen, Jackson, Fairman, and Deming died in Lafayette. Many of the others removed to other localities. Dr. Clark served one year in the House, and eight years in the Senate of the State Legislature—was appointed under the administration of Harrison and Tyler, with Lot Bloomfield and Jonathan McCarty, to examine accounts under the treaty with the Miami Indians in 1841; and was elected and served as a member of the Convention to revise the Constitution of Indiana, which convened at Indianapolis in 1851, acquitting himself as an able and faithful representative, and honest man, in all the various responsible trusts in which he was called to act.

Dr. Deming was an able and eloquent man, and in point of talents would rank favorably with any of his political and professional compeers. He served one term in the Legislature of Indiana, and filled important chairs in two Medical Colleges in this State. He was afterwards elected and served in the chair of Theory and Practice in the Medical University of Missouri, at St. Louis, which position he occupied at the time of his death, in February, 1855.

Drs. Jennings and Jewett have long since acquired a high reputation for their professional skill and industry, enjoy good health, have an extensive practice, and have accumulated a competency of this world's goods. Jewett is wealthy.

On the Wea prairie were Drs. John Durkee, Harry L. Doubleday, and Paris Mendenhall, all of whom were esteemed skillful physicians, and worthy members of society. All three died long since. At Fairfield (now Dayton) lived Drs. Horrom, John S. Davis, Fullenwider, and James Gentry, who was killed, many years ago, near Dayton, by his horse running away with him, and throwing him against a tree which stood in the Wild Cat bottom, some half mile east of Dayton. John S. Davis alone remains, at Dayton, in the practice, with a wide and well deserved reputation as a physician and a man. At Americus resided Dr. Anthony Garret, now located at Delphi; and west of the Wabash river were the Drs. Conduits, who remained but a few years in Tippecanoe county.

In giving a brief notice of the clergy of the different Christian denominations, who have officiated in Lafayette, I will first make mention of the Methodist, which built the first house of worship in Lafayette. Their Methodist system of itinerancy, allowing their ministers to remain generally but one year, or, at most, but two years, in a place, will swell the list of their preachers to an extent almost equal to the number of the whole of the other denominations put together. I shall not attempt to give their names, nor the time occupied by their ministrations in chronological order, and I am not sure that I will recollect all their names. Rev. Hackaliah Vredenburg preached the first Methodist sermon in Lafayette, or, at least, was the first circuit rider who held meeting in the newly laid out village. Henry Buell, Eli Farmer, Stephen R. Beggs, James Armstrong, and John Strange, all preached in Lafayette prior to the year 1831. They were succeeded by Samuel C. Cooper and Samuel Brenton, who were followed by Boyd Phelps and Wesley Woods;—the latter died soon after he entered upon the circuit, and was succeeded by S. R. Ball. In 1832–33 Richard Hargrave and Nehemiah Griffith rode the Lafayette circuit, and James L. Thompson was presiding elder. Griffith was an ardent, devoted minister, and wore himself out in the service of his Master, in early life. As a revivalist, he was almost if not quite as successful as Armstrong, and the lamented Edwin Ray, who both, like himself, died in the morning of life, with their armor on. Hargrave was an able and eloquent preacher, who often carried away his audience by the irresistible charms of his copious, flowing eloquence. He still lives, and enjoys a green old age, ready to work on in the cause of his Master, or go to his reward whenever called for. William M. Clark and Wm. Watson were next on the list. Clark still lives in Knox county, Illinois, and has became quite wealthy. I heard him preach an able and telling sermon last Summer, at a camp meeting held near the town of Henderson, a few miles north of Galesburg, Illinois. At the conference of 1835, Lafayette was formed into a station, and Dr. H. S. Talbot was appointed the first stationed preacher for two years. He was succeeded by Lorenzo B. Smith, John A. Brouse, and Hawley B. Beers, each of whom remained one year. In 1840–41, Amasa Johnson took charge and remained two years. He was a bold, original and effective speaker. He died in Fort Wayne several years ago, beloved by all who knew him. He was succeeded by H. B. Beers and Jacob M. Stallard, who each remained one year. In 1844-45, Samuel Brenton was sent to Lafayette station, where he remained two years, and was succeeded by John H. Hull (the present incumbent of the Western Charge), who remained one year. He was succeeded by C. M. Boyd, who remained two years, and T. S. Webb, one year. About this time Aaron Wood was presiding elder of this district. In 1848, W. F. Wheeler (who recently died) was stationed as a City Missionary, and through his labors the nucleus of a second Charge was formed. At the conference in 1850, the church was divided in Western and Eastern Charges. The Western Charge being the original church, had in 1850–51 Rev. John Daniels, now of California conference, placed over it, and the Eastern Charge had Rev. T. S. Webb placed over it, with Rev. Joseph Marsee presiding elder, who lives at Indianapolis, superannuated. The subsequent ministers stationed at the Western Charge were as follows: In 1851 –52, G. W. Beswick, who died at Greencastle a few years since; —1852–53, J. M. Stallard, two years—1854–55, S. R. Ball, part of the year, and E. D. Whitten the balance. Benjamin Winans, presiding elder. In 1855–56, George W. Crawford, two years, who has recently passed to his reward, in the morning of his life and usefulness. In 1857–58, A. A. Gee, who was succeeded by J. H. Hull. John L. Smith, presiding elder, who at the present time (with his colleagues, J. M. Stallard, Richard Hargrave, and James Johnson) is attending the General Conference of the United States, now in session in the city of Buffalo, and will, in all probability, be chosen a Bishop—which office his talents and long and efficient services, eminently quality him to fill. This Charge numbers over two hundred members—has a large and flourishing Sabbath School, and a valuable and interesting library.

The Eastern Charge was organized by setting off to it one hundred and forty members from the old or Western Church. Its second minister was William Graham, in 1851; Luther Taylor, in 1852; G. M. Boyd, in 1853–54; W. F. Wheeler, in 1855; John Leach, in 1856; in 1857–58, James C. Reed, and in 1859–60, N. L. Brakeman, the present incumbent. Connected with this Charge is also a large and flourishing Sabbath School, with a valuable library. The number of members in this Charge in the year 1859, was two hundred and five, as shown in Hawes'

Directory of the City of Lafayette, to which I am indebted for much valuable data in regard to the organization of the various churches in Lafayette; as also the Church Records of the Western Charge. Both Charges have large, commodious brick chapels.

I regret that my restricted limits prevent me from giving a more extended notice of Aaron Wood, Allen Wylie, George M. Beswick, J. M. Stallard, and others above mentioned, whose talents and efficient services in the ministry entitle them to the warm regard of all lovers of genuine religion and sound morality.

The German Methodist Episcopal Church was organized in Lafayette in 1851, under the pastoral care of Rev. C. Kellar. It has since been under the charge of Rev. J. Barth, T. B. Baker, F. Shroek, S. Barth, J. Kishing, and J. H. Fusz. Their house of worship is in the eastern portion of the city. Number of members, over fifty.

The second church organized in Lafayette was by the Presbyterian denomination, on the 26th day of May, 1828. Their first minister was the Rev. James Crawford. He was assisted occasionally by Rev. James Thompson, from Crawfordsville. In May, 1830, the services of Rev. James A. Carnahan (now of Dayton, in this county) were procured. He was succeeded by Rev. Michael Hummer, in 1834. Rev. Joseph G. Wilson was the next pastor, and remained as such until in May, 1837, when the "Exscinding Acts" were passed by the General Assembly of the Presbyterian Church, which caused the division of the Church into Old School and New School. With the latter of these bodies the Rev. Mr. Wilson and several members of the Church sympathized. Those who adhered to the Old School Assembly refused to commune with them, or recognize them as a part of the Presbyterian Church. In 1839, the Second Presbyterian Church was organized, under the pastoral care of Rev. Joseph G. Wilson. In 1840, Rev. E. W. Wright was called to the pastoral care of the First or Old School Church, where he remained until in 1845. He was succeeded by S. H. Hazzard and P. R. Vannatta. In 1850, Rev. I. N. Candee, now of the city of Galesburg, Illinois, was called to the office of pastor, and continued until in 1855, when he was dismissed at his own request. He was succeeded by W. W. Colemary, who remained about eighteen months in the discharge of his pastoral duties, when he vacated the charge on account of ill health. He was succeeded by Rev. R. H. Allen, late Secretary of the American Sunday School Union, who still continues as the pastor of the Old School congregation, who have a superb new brick chapel, on the corner of Columbia and Missouri streets. Number of communicants, about one hundred.

Rev. Mr. Wilson continued as pastor of the New School Church in Lafayette until in May, 1849, when he was succeeded by Rev. Charles F. Marshall, who remained until in May, 1857. In October, 1857, Rev. Charles Wiley, D. D., was called to the pastoral charge of this Church, and was succeeded by Rev. Daniel Rice, the present incumbent. The chapel of this congregation, on the corner of Main and Missouri streets, is a large and splendid Gothic structure, being fifty-four feet wide, and ninety-eight feet long—is beautifully and conveniently finished, and is scarcely excelled, as a house of worship, by any in the State. Connected with it is a large and flourishing Sabbath School, which has a very efficient organization, and fine library of choice works. Number of communicants, about seventy-five.

The Associate Reform Presbyterian Church was organized in 1842, and called Rev. Samuel Finlay as pastor, who remained about one year. Afterwards Rev. James H. Peacock; after him Rev. David A. Carnahan, Rev. Mr. Hoyt, and Rev. J. N. Pressley, who removed a few years since to Indianola, Iowa, since whose removal the Church has been without a regular pastor, but have had the service of stated and occasional supplies. Their chapel is on Ferry, between Missouri and Pearl streets. Connected with this Church is a flourishing Sabbath School. Number of communicants, about sixty.

The Baptist Church in Lafayette was organized in 1832, under the pastoral charge of Dr. Loyal Fairman, who was succeeded by Rev. Simon G. Minor, now of Canton, Illinois, under whose faithful labors many members were added to the Church, and a fine brick chapel was built on Missouri, between Main and Ferry streets. Mr. Minor was succeeded by a Mr. French, who, after remaining a short time pastor of the Church, was succeeded by Rev. Anson Tucker, who was subsequently stationed at Monmouth, Illinois, where he died. Mr. Tucker was succeeded by Rev. T. L. Breckinridge, whose pastoral labors have lately been terminated on account of his ill health. The congregation is large, and connected with the Church is a very large and flourishing Sabbath School, with a fine and valuable library.

The Protestant Episcopal Church, called St. John's Church, was organized March 27, 1837, by Rev. Samuel, R. Johnson, in connection with Wm. M. Jenners, Robert Jones, Sr., John D. Smith, Jasper Bradley, and Dr. Elizur Deming, who composed the first vestry. Rev. S. R. Johnson, was a man of great piety and benevolence. Possessing a large fortune, and feeling responsible for the manner in which he used it, he was constant and liberal in his acts of beneficence—carrying temporal and spiritual consolation not only to the suffering and destitute of his own parish, but wherever he saw suffering humanity, his warm, impulsive heart gave responsive throbs, and his liberal hand supplied the needed aid. He not only donated a large and valuable lot of ground on the corner of Missouri and Ferry streets, to the society to build a chapel on, but he also built a small frame house for worship, mostly at his own expense, and for many years discharged the duties of rector of the parish, without charge. In return for such liberality on his part, his congregation erected and presented him with a splendid brick house, worth three thousand dollars. Many instances of his acts of liberality might be given, showing the characteristic benevolence of the man, but for want of space I will relate one only:

One night he caught a man emerging from his cellar with a ham of bacon. Mortified and astounded at the daring theft, the minister sharply reprimanded him for such conduct. Abner, for that was the christian name of the transgressor, to excuse himself for this act of rapacity, said that his family was in a state of starvation, occasioned by the severe and protracted affliction of its members—that he did not wish to disturb the evening devotions of the benevolent minister—that he had taken the ham with the intention of telling him of it, and paying for it when he became able. The clergyman relented—took him back into his cellar and gave him an additional bacon ham, telling him whenever in future he needed provisions for his family, to call on him, and dismissed him with his blessing and prayer to the Almighty to grant all needed aid, temporal and spiritual, to the needy, afflicted man and his family. On returning into his house, he said: "Dear wife, we must immediately send some flour over to Abner W—'s

—his family is in much want, and I fear we have committed great sin, in letting the poor go unprovided for, who live within a stone's throw of our house." The flour, and other dainties, such as the parson and his kind spouse well knew how to select for the indigent, were carried over to the poor man's cabin, and the man of God felt satisfied that his philanthropy had not been misapplied. But the obdurate and ungrateful Abner still continued to rob cellars and hen-roosts, and carry on a kind of promiscuous stealing, until he was finally arrested and committed to the State prison for stealing fifty dollars in silver from a friend and guest.

After remaining in charge of St. John's Church in Lafayette for many years, the condition of his business affairs in the city of Brooklyn, New York, imperiously demanded his presence and attention there, and accordingly in June, 1847, he resigned, and was succeeded in the rectorship by Rev. J. W. McCullough, D. D., who remained until in March, 1849. Rev. A. M. Lautrelle officiated for a short time. On February, 25, 1850, Right Rev. George Upfold, D. D., Bishop of the Diocese of Indiana, was invited to the rectorship of the Church, and remained in that capacity until January, 1851, when he resigned to devote his undivided attention to his Episcopal duties. Rev. John O. Barton was rector from the time of the Bishop's resignation until June, 1856, when W. P. Ray was called as rector, and resigned July 1, 1857. In September, 1857, Rev. Anthony TenBroeck was called to the rectorship, and served until in September, 1859, since which time, the Church has had no regular minister. This congregation has a large and splendid new brick chapel, on the corner of Missouri and Ferry streets. Number of communicants, one hundred and twenty-seven. There is a large and flourishing Sabbath School connected with this Church, provided with a large and select library.

The Roman Catholic Church (English), known as the Church of St. Mary and St. Martha, was organized in 1837, and was supplied by Father Francis, from Logansport. The present Church building, which is of brick, forty by eighty feet in size, situated on the corner of Brown and Mississippi streets, cost $10,000. There is also a brick school house on the lot, and a school taught in it. The membership, including children, is over twenty-five hundred. The priests who have officiated here have been Father Francis, Father Clark, Father Maloney, and Father Kilroy, the present incumbent.

The Church of St. Bonifaceus (German Roman Catholic), situated on the corner of Chesnut and Ferry streets, was organized in 1853. The building is brick, and cost $7,000. There is also a school house and residence for the priest, erected on the Church lot. Father Stephens is the priest who officiates, and is quite an eloquent and effective speaker.

The Christian Church was organized in 1849. They have a commodious brick chapel on Missouri street, between North and Brown. Rev. John Longley was the venerable and venerated pastor of this Church for many years. H. St. John Vandake was pastor for the year 1845. Rev. Joseph Franklin is the present pastor, assisted occasionally by the aged and beloved pastor above alluded to. Present number of members, about ninety-five. Connected with this Church there is a flourishing Sabbath School.

The Unitarian Church meets for worship at Melodeon Hall. I have not learned the name of their minister, nor the number of their members.

The United Brethren Church was early organized in Lafayette. They have a fine brick chapel, about thirty-five by forty-five feet, with a basement, on Pearl street, in the northern portion of the city. Their ministers have been John Peters, Andrew Wimsett, Bailey, and Hamilton, their present presiding elder; Rev. David Brown, James Davis (long since gone to his reward), James Griffith, and others, have at different times preached for the congregation.

The German Lutheran Church was organized in 1848, by Rev. A. Leemhous. The following year they purchased a lot on Ferry street, between Pearl and Clark, where they erected a neat frame chapel. Connected with this Church is a German and English school. Membership, over 40. Rev. Frederick Koenig is pastor.

The Universalist Church is a fine, large frame building, situated on the corner of Main and Clark streets, which cost $3,000. The first pastor was Erasmus Manford, now of St. Louis. He was succeeded by Phineas Hathaway, who done much to build up the Church and congregation, and Rev. I. M. Westfall, the present minister.

The Jewish Synagogue was organized in February, 1851,

under the name of "Ahvas Achim," or Loving Brothers. Rabbi Loventhal officiated for several years. They are supplied by occasional Rabbis, from Cincinnati, Chicago, and other points. Connected with the Synagogue there is a flourishing school, in which the children are taught Hebrew, German, and the first principles of their religion. The membership is about thirty-three, and there are no better citizens than form the Jewish population of this city. The different Rabbis who have officiated here have been Rev. Goodman, Emmich, Loventhal, and Shoenberg, their present priest.

CHAPTER XIX.

NARRATIVE OF THE CAPTIVITY BY THE INDIANS, OF RICHARD RUE, GEORGE HOLMAN, AND IRVIN HINTON.

On the 11th day of February, 1781, a wagoner by the name of Irvin Hinton, was sent from a blockhouse at the village of Louisville, at the Falls of the Ohio river, to Harrodsburg, for a load of provisions for the fort. Two young men, named Richard Rue and George Holman, the former aged nineteen years, and the latter sixteen, were sent as guards to protect the wagon from the depredations of any hostile Indians that might be lurking in the canebrakes or ravines through which they had to pass in going to and returning from Harrodsburg. There had been no late reasons for apprehending danger from the Indians so early in the season, although there was a general expectation that about the time the leaves were as large as a squirrel's ear, there would be a general attack on the frontier inhabitants of Virginia, Pennsylvania, and Kentucky.

Soon after the party set out on their journey, a severe snow storm set in, which continued with unabated fury until after noon, filling the wagon ruts, and wreathing the copse and canebrakes in a rich white robe, until mother earth appeared to lie prone in a winding-sheet of spotless purity. Lest the melting snow might dampen the powder in their rifles, the guards fired them off, intending to reload them as soon as the storm ceased. Hinton urged on his horses, while Rue walked briskly a few rods ahead of the wagon, and Holman about the same distance behind. As they ascended a hill about eight miles from Louisville, Hinton heard some one say "ho" to the horses. Supposing that something was wrong about the wagon, he stopped, looked around and asked Holman why he called to him to halt. Holman said that he had not spoken. Hinton then said: "Rue, was it you that cried 'ho'?" Rue replied in the negative, but said that he heard the voice distinctly, and supposed that it was Holman, or himself, that had spoken.

At this time a voice cried out, "I will solve the mystery for you. It was Simon Girty that cried 'ho!' and he meant what he said!" at the same time emerging from a sink-hole a few rods from the roadside, followed by thirteen Indians, who immediately surrounded the three Kentuckians, and demanded them to surrender, or die instantly. Rue instinctively raised his gun to his face to shoot down Girty, but on remembering that it was empty, he took it down, and the little party, making a virtue of necessity, at once surrendered to this renegade white man and his Indian allies. Being so near two forts, Girty made all possible speed in making fast his prisoners. He stripped the harness from the horses, selecting the lines, and such ropes and leathern straps as might be needed on the journey, and prepared for an immediate flight across the Ohio river. After securely binding the prisoners, by passing ropes under one arm and over the opposite shoulder, they cut off the legs of their pantaloons about four inches above the knee, and started them off through the deep snow, as fast as the horses could trot—leaving the wagon, containing a few empty barrels, standing in the road. A tall Shawnee warrior rode one of the best of Hinton's team horses, and led Rue as his captive. A Delaware Chief rode another of the horses, leading Holman with a portion of the lines with which the wagoner had guided his lead horses. Hinton, although he had a wife and six children, whom he had that morning left at the Falls, was likewise put into leading-strings, and hurried along after a fierce-looking Shawnee, mounted upon another of his horses. The remaining horse Simon Girty, the generalissimo of the band, appropriated to his own use, alternately dashing along at the head of the company, then falling back and talking with the prisoners, whom he told if they valued their lives, they must keep profound silence, and make no attempt to escape. The party arrived at the Ohio river before dark that evening, where three large bark canoes were secreted in a cove on the south bank of the river, some twelve miles above the Falls. The prisoners, weary and benumbed with cold, were placed in one of the canoes, under the care of Girty and their respective captors, and two other Indians, who paddled the canoe. The rest of the Indians brought over the other crafts, swimming the horses over by the lower side and stern of the canoes.

After crossing the Ohio river, the prisoners were hurried with great speed into the wilderness of the North-Western Territory, towards Wa-puc-ca-nat-ta. The party made no halt until late the first night, when they encamped without striking a fire, about half a mile from the trace, some twenty miles north of the Ohio river. Here a brief parley was held between Girty and the Indians, in which the point was discussed, whether it would not be best for the party, in order to elude pursuit, to strike immediately for the Indian town at Vincennes, on the Wabash river. Girty and a few of the party were in favor of hastening to Vincennes, while the majority were of the opinion that it would be safest to proceed at once to Wa-puc-ca-nat-ta. Finally it was decided to make a feint by traveling awhile in the direction of Vincennes, then change their course and steer through the White river country to the Auglaize.

At dawn next morning the party were threading the wilderness, in the direction of the town on the Wabash, with precipitate haste, keeping a spy a few hundred yards in advance of the main body, and another about as far in the rear. They traveled late the second night also, diverging about as far from the path as they did the previous night, and encamped again without striking a fire—a precaution always observed by the Indians on marches of this kind, to prevent any pursuing party finding their encampment, and surprising them while asleep. On retiring to rest each night, the invariable rule was to place the captives in the middle, with their hands tied behind them, and then a large, active Indian was placed on each side, with tomahawks within reach,

8

so that if an attack was made on them in the night, they would be ready to meet an invading foe, or dispatch the prisoners, if about to be rescued by their friends.

Girty was morose and taciturn. The few words he spoke were generally in the Delaware language. Rue had been in several campaigns against the Indians, and had obtained a smattering of several of the Indian dialects. Girty at length thought he could perceive by the shades that passed over Rue's countenance at times, that he was not entirely ignorant of the Indian language, and took occasion during his temporary absence (which he artfully contrived for the purpose), to enquire of his fellow captives if he had not been in some of the campaigns and battles against the Indians. They were admonished to tell the truth—that if the Indians ever caught them in a lie, death would be the inevitable consequence. They hesitated giving an answer. The question was pressed with a menacing flourish of the tomahawk. They replied that he had been in several campaigns against the Indians. How many? Three or four, was the response. Rue chanced to overhear this colloquy. He thought his hour had come. But knowing that bravery was esteemed one of the highest virtues by the savages, he approached the camp fire as if he knew nothing of what had transpired, sat down his brass kettle of water he had been ordered to bring, and took a seat on a log by the side of Girty, in a quiet, confident manner. The old bogus savage appeared moody. At length he muttered out, "Rue, was you ever out in a campaign against the Indians?" "Yes, I was." "How many?" "Four," replied the captive. "Was you with General Clark at the taking of Vincennes?" "Yes." "Was you with him when he made his dash against Chillicothe, and destroyed the Piqua towns and Loramie's store?" "I was," was the ready reply. At this Girty sprung from the log, rage convulsed his whole frame, while with a ghastly frown he muttered: "You played h—l there! didn't you! I have a mind to split your skull with this hatchet!" but he changed the weapon in his hand, and struck the prisoner a blow on the head with the handle.

Simon Girty was a white man, a Pennsylvanian by birth. He was brave, ambitious, and unscrupulous. He espoused the cause of the Indians (whose prisoner he had been for many years, in

his early boyhood), and led them to many bloody massacres of
his white brethren. From the time of his treacherous apostacy,
he vied with the most cruel and relentless savages to circumvent
his old friends, and put them to death by the most cruel and
ingenious tortures. He was present at the burning of Colonel
Crawford, and several other brave soldiers; and so far from
attempting to save them from the most excruciating death, he
coolly looked on, with a demoniac satisfaction, and told them
that they were but getting their just deserts.

The prisoners had heard of his unparalleled cruelty, and from
the time it was announced they were the captives of Simon
Girty, they felt that they were subject to the caprice of a cruel
and bloodthirsty man, who would kill or spare, as interest or
passion might dictate. The dastardly blow he had given Rue
over the head with his tomahawk handle, accompanied by a volley
of curses, tended to increase the settled hatred and disgust of the
captives, who were forced to conceal their dislike as much as
possible, and affect a feeling of contentment, when they expected
every hour that some one, or all of them, might feel the edge
instead of the handle of the tomahawk, which was often brandished over their heads through sheer wantonness of their brutal
captors.

The third day after crossing the Ohio, the party, finding that
they were not pursued, relaxed their speed, and turned aside for
the purpose of brousing their horses, and resting themselves and
their prisoners, who were all much fatigued by the forced marches,
and lack of rest, the two preceding days and nights.

Their scanty store of provisions having given out, hunters
were sent out, who, after a few hours' absence, returned with a
small deer and two turkeys. These were dressed and hastily
broiled on the coals, without salt, and were divided out among the
company. Turtle soup, or cooked frogs, would not have been a
more savory dish to a Frenchman, than were these fragments of
wild game to the famished, travel-worn prisoners; who now felt
they were beyond the reach of aid from their friends, and were
doomed to a fearful captivity, among exasperated savages, who
considered themselves and the whole Indian race trampled upon
and abused by the steady and systematic encroachments of the
white man, who had driven them from the shores of the Atlantic

across the Alleghanies, and were seeking to drive them west of the Mississippi river. The prisoners remembered the cruel circumvention and cold blooded murder a few years before, of the noble Cornstalk, a leading Chief of the Shawnees, his brave son Ellinipsico, and the young Chief Red Hawk, near the mouth of the Great Kanhawa, and did not know but they might be the three victims that would be sacrificed to appease the manes of these lamented chieftains.

From this point the party changed their course for Wa-puc-ca-nat-ta, passing through the White river and Blue river countries, crossing the head waters of the Wabash east of where Fort Wayne was afterwards built. On arriving within a day's journey of Wa-puc-ca-nat-ta, on the Auglaize, a runner was dispatched to inform the Indians of the return of Girty and his party, and to make preparations to have the prisoners run the gauntlet on entering the town. When the party had arrived within a few miles of the town, they were met by several Chiefs and warriors, who come out to do themselves the honor of meeting the return-ing band, and assist in arranging the preliminaries of the gauntlet, a time-honored custom of the savages. A brief parley ensued. Girty called the prisoners before him. He told them that within a few hours they would arrive at the village, where they would find the Indians drawn up in two lines, one line on each side of the path, for two or three hundred yards from the council-house. They must pass between these two lines of warriors, who would strike at them with clubs and knives as they passed. If they were knocked down, it was against the rule to hit them while down. They must get upon their feet again, and run for the council-room with all speed. When they gained the goal, they were free from further assaults. There they would be tried for their lives. If the council thought it best to spare their lives, they would so decide. If they were condemned to death, the council would determine the time and manner of their execution.

On arriving within sight of the village, they saw the lines drawn up on either side of the path, and the grim, painted sav-ages awaiting the approach of the prisoners.

It was decided that Hinton should first run the gauntlet. He received severe whacks and blows over the head and shoulders, from the clubs and sides of the tomahawks of the Indians, before he reached the council-house, which afforded much sport to the Indians, who evinced their hilarity in the most vociferous yells, and roars of laughter. After a few more hasty directions from Girty, as to the rules of the race, and in what manner he must behave himself in the different phases of the chase, Rue was next started down between the lines, and an Indian after him with an uplifted tomahawk. He far outstripped his pursuer, dodged most of the blows aimed at him as he passed, and gained the council-house amidst the noisy shouts of the savages.

Holman was reluctant to enter the race. He told Girty that he would not be able to pass through so severe an ordeal—that he thought it unfair to put a stripling like himself, wasted with famine, and worn down with hardships, to so severe a test. A pow-wow was held. The programme was changed. The men retired from the lines, and their places were filled by squaws and boys, with knives, clubs and switches in their hands. A comical smile played upon the faces of all but Holman, who was started down the lines, followed by an Indian with a long switch. The chase was spirited. Switches and clubs rattled over his head, shoulders and body, as he darted between the lines to the council-house, amidst the loud and prolonged whoops and *ha ha's* of old and young, who looked upon the last race as the lighter after-piece or farce, that succeeded the weightier tragedy, relaxing the stern visage of war, and extracting a laugh from the sombre Chief of a dozen battles, and the wearer of twice as many scalps.

The feast was spread. Chiefs and warriors partook of the bountiful repast. The prisoners were supplied with food, and told to await with patience the decision of the council, which would that afternoon decide their fate.

The savage sanhedrim was soon in session. An old dark-visaged Chief presided. Speech after speech was made, during which many violent gestures were made, and angry glances cast toward the corner of the room where the prisoners sat, which boded no good to the unfortunate trio, who understood but little of their harangues. The council broke up. The prisoners were told that their cases were not finally disposed of, but were continued for the presence of other Chiefs and warriors, who lived on the Scioto and Big Miami, who were expected to arrive in a few days.

Hinton's mind was filled with gloomy forebodings of a cruel fate impending over him. He thought he saw in the trial (which had been continued for the presence of other chieftains, equally, and perhaps more cruel than those who had sat in the former council) unmistakeable signs of a hard fate. Visions of his wife and children at home, were in his slumbers by night, and filled his thoughts by day. Could he escape from the ruthless savages, and again press those loved ones to his bosom? Or, must he passively await whatever doom they might determine to inflict upon him? were questions that constantly presented themselves to him. He cautiously whispered his feelings and intentions to his fellow captives, who could only sympathize with him in his manifold sorrows. He said that the affection he bore for his wife and children would impel him to desert upon the first opportunity. He knew that the chances of escape were greatly against him—that if he was recaptured he would be killed forthwith, without doubt. His fellow prisoners remonstrated against his attempting to escape, as hazardous in the extreme. They advised him to remain with them and abide the trial—that some circumstance might transpire to their advantage. But Hinton was determined in his plans, which were kept entirely secret, and a few nights afterward it was announced that "Red Head," as the Indians called him, had escaped, taking with him an Indian's gun and accoutrements. There was a general flashing of eyes and tomahawks around the encampment. "Look well to the other prisoners," broke from many savage lips, while menacing words and gestures evinced how deep was their chagrin at the unexpected escape of the prisoner, whom they least expected meditated such a thing. From the first day of his captivity, Hinton affected a quiet, stoical indifference, and appeared to be the most docile and happy one of the three. The advantages of age and experience enabled him to school his feelings and hide his real intentions, so that his sudden exit struck the whole village like a clap of thunder from a clear sky. Pursuit was immediately instituted. Scores of infuriated savages thronged the woods in every direction to find some trace of the fleeing fugitive, who it was supposed would aim for the Falls of the Ohio, but as a matter of precaution might in the outset start in some other direction to elude pursuit.

A stricter guard was placed over the remaining prisoners, who were plainly told that should they attempt to escape, and fail to do so, they would immediately be put to death, and they could not promise in how mild or severe a manner; that Hinton's escape had exasperated the tribes, and that the two remaining prisoners would most likely receive less clemency at their pending trial.

Next morning the most of the pursuers returned. Some eight or ten only had pressed on to a point where they expected to intercept Hinton on his way to the Ohio river. They were right in their calculations, for late in the afternoon of the second day after his escape, a man was seen gliding through the woods about half a mile from the trace that led from Sandusky to the old Chillicothe town. At times he would stop, and from some log or high piece of ground overlook the surrounding country, as if he were a spy. Thus he walked into the midst of an ambuscade of his wiley pursuers, who, after watching his motions for awhile, crawled from one hiding place to another until they had completely invested him, before he was aware of danger. They uttered a simultaneous and prolonged yell, and rushed upon the lone, fatigued traveler, whom they recognized to be Hinton, firing two or three shots as they pressed around him, without any other effect than increasing his consternation at his truly appalling condition. He was seized and disarmed, and told to prepare for a cruel death; that they had often admonished him of the danger of attempting to escape, and that "Indians would not lie"—they would be found as good as their word; that night he would be burned at the stake, that the severity of his punishment might deter others from attempting an escape. He told them that he did not care so much for his own life; that it was his love for his wife and children in Kentucky that caused him to break away from his captivity; that as for himself, he could soon have become reconciled to their mode of life, and made himself happy by hunting and fishing. His touching appeal to the heart of the husband and father, in behalf of the dear ones far away whose welfare now caused a deeper solicitude than his own desperate condition, failed to excite the sympathy of his inexorable captors, who immediately set about making preparations to burn their devoted victim. He earnestly implored them to shoot or tomahawk him, and not protract his sufferings unnecessarily; but they turned a deaf ear to his entreaties, and consummated their arrangements for his death. After partaking of their evening repast, which they shared with their fatigued and hungry victim, they drove a stake into the ground in the center of a circle of dry sticks and brush which they had gathered for the purpose. They then proceeded to strip and black the prisoner —a preliminary usually attended to in such sacrifices. After tying the prisoner to the stake, burning faggots were applied to the brush in several places; the war-whoop thrilled through the dark surrounding forest like the chorus of a band of infernal spirits escaped from Pandemonium, and the scalp-dance was struck up by those demons in human shape, who for hours encircled the roasting victim brandishing their tomahawks and war-clubs, and venting their indignant execrations on the helpless sufferer, who meekly submitted to his immolation, and died about midnight from the effects of the slow intense heat, which literally roasted him to death. As soon as he fell upon the ground, the Indian who first discovered him that evening in the woods sprang in, sunk his tomahawk into his skull above the ear, and with his knife stripped off the scalp, which he bore back with him to the town as a trophy, and which was tauntingly thrust into the faces of Rue and Holman, with the interrogation, "Can you smell the fire on the scalp of your old red-headed friend?—We cooked him and left him for the wolves to make a breakfast upon: that is the way we serve runaway prisoners."

Shortly after the cruel murder of Hinton, a deputation arrived from Detroit, stating that the contemplated movement against the whites on the Kentucky borders had been postponed; that calls had been made for a general rendevous of the Indians at Detroit; and for those at Wa-puc-ca-nat-ta, Chillicothe, and intervening points to come on, bringing with them any captives they might have in their possession. Girty and his party, with the principal portion of the warriors then at Wa-puc-ca-nat-ti, took up their march for the point designated. At the end of the third day's march, the party approached an Indian village situated on the Maumee River, a few miles above the spot where the city of Toledo now stands. It was determined that the prisoners should be made to run the gauntlet again at this place; and as the Chillicothe Chiefs, and those residing at the Mad River towns were present, it was determined that the postponed trial of Rue and Holman should be brought to a final conclusion. A general halt was made. Their approach was heralded to the town. The usual lines of painted savages were drawn up on either side of the path. The order of the chase was the same as at Wa-puc-ca-nat-ti, except that Holman's portion was not diluted with women and switches. A tall, active Indian was placed behind Rue with an old sword in his hand. At the given signal Rue darted down the line, receiving many blows from the clubs and hatchets of the Indians in the line, which stunned him so that his pursuer overtook him and hit him a couple of severe strokes over the head, which well nigh felled him to the ground. At this point he had reached a brush fence that enclosed several angles of the village, and, making a bound, cleared the fence and alighted on the other side; but finding his pursuer had crossed the fence at almost the same instant of time, Rue affected to stumble and fall to the ground. The Indian waved the sword over his head and motioned for him to get up and run. The prisoner laid still. The Indian stepped off eight or ten paces, and again told him to get up and run. The prostrate prisoner motioned with his hand for him to get back over the brush fence, which the Indian did, Rue feigning inability to proceed. The Indian with the sword then walked back some ten or twelve paces from the fence, and urged the prisoner to run. As nimble as a cat Rue sprang from the ground, and darted into the council house before his pursuer could get within ten paces of him, amidst the deafening yells of the savages, who seemed to admire the stratagem used to avoid the ponderous blows of his pursuer. Holman was then passed down the lines, and made the goal with about as much flagellation as his savage tormentors thought he would be able to bear.

The usual feast was then spread. After the feast was over, the Chiefs and warriors indulged in the scalp dance, which the prisonoers regarded as an ill omen to precede the council that was to decide their fate for weal or for woe. The dance ended. The grim warriors seated themselves in a circle around a prominent Chief, who rose and harrangued them for several minutes in an animated style and then took his seat. One Chief and warrior after another rose and addressed the council, until all the chief dignitaries had spoken. At times the debate became quite stormy, and it was with difficulty the presiding sachem could keep order.

The vote was finally taken, and it was evident to the prisoners that a hard verdict had been rendered against them. The glances, gestures, and general demeanor of the council spoke the language of doom. In about a quarter of an hour after the council broke up, Girty informed the prisoners of their impending fate. The council had decided that they should be burned at the stake that night. The necessary preparations were made—dry sticks and brush were gathered and piled around in two circles, in the center of which a stake was firmly driven into the ground. The faces and hands of the two prisoners were blackened in the customary manner, and as the evening approached the two doomed young men sat looking upon the setting sun for the last time, as the golden orb seemed to settle down behind the distant tree tops, throwing back a radiant smile upon the ruddy clouds, as if to remind the sufferers of that brighter sphere which awaits the spirits of the just, after they have passed through the dark valley of the shadow of death—whether that death be by fire, water, or lingering disease.

They prayed earnestly to God to turn aside the horrid fate that awaited them, if consistent with His divine will—that all power in heaven and earth belonged to Him—that He who had sustained Daniel in the den of lions, and the three Hebrew children in the fiery furnace, could turn the hearts of these fierce savages, and melt them to pity. But, if it was not consistent with His will to avert the impeding death, to prepare their souls for heaven and immortal happiness, and fill their hearts with fortitude to pass through the fiery ordeal with firmness and resignation.

An unusual excitement appeared to run through the fragments of the assembly, that lingered around the council house. High words and angry looks evinced a want of unanimity among the different tribes that composed the assembly. What was the cause of the dissatisfaction the prisoners could not learn, nor could they ascertain that it had any connection with the sentence in their case. At a pause in the contention, a noble looking Indian approached where the prisoners were sitting, and spoke a few words in the Mingo language to the guards. He then took Holman by the hand, lifted him to his feet, cut the cords that bound him to his fellow prisoner, caused the black to be taken off his

face and hands, put his hand kindly upon his head, and said :—
" I adopt you as my son, to fill the place of one I have lately buried—you are now a kinsman of Logan, 'the white man's friend,'
as he has been called, but who has lately proven himself to be a
terrible avenger of the wrongs inflicted upon him by the bloody
Cresap and his men.   Girty, with evident reluctance, interpreted
what he said.   Holman felt that his prayer was answered, as far
as concerned his own safety, and he almost fell to the ground at
the sudden and unexpected announcement of his deliverance. But
the sad fate that awaited his companion, neutralized his excess
of joy, and he felt that life itself would be dear, if he had to witness the excruciating torture and death of his friend, whom he
loved as a brother.

The commutation of Holman's sentence, and the adoption of
him into a family nearly related to Logan, sent a momentary
thrill of pleasure through the breast of Rue, who, although doomed to die in a few hours, still entertained a faint hope that
something might transpire to avert, or at least postpone his doom :
and should he even that night suffer at the stake, his friend might
be spared to tell at some future time of the sad fate of Hinton
and himself.

After a brief interval, two Indians approached Rue with leathern thongs in their hands, cut loose the cords that bound his feet,
raised him from the ground, stripped him, passed a cord under
one arm and over the opposite shoulder, which they tied securely ;
around this they passed the long, coiled leathern strap, and made
it fast.   These were regarded as the notes of preparation for the
burning, and Holman and Rue embraced each other most affectionately, with a sorrow too deep for utterance or description,
which would have melted less obdurate hearts to pity.

Rue was then led to one of the stakes in the center of the circle of dried brushwood to which he was tied fast.   At this time
a general contention pervaded the encampment—not a few tomahawks were brandished in the air, and scores of knives were
seen glittering in the hands of exasperated Indians, who seemed
to be in a general ferment.

Just as the lighted faggots were about to be applied to the dry
brush that encircled the devoted prisoner, a tall, active young Shawnee, a son of the victim's captor, sprang into the ring, and, with

his tomahawk, chopped off the cord that bound him to the stake, led him out of the ring amidst the deafening plaudits of a part of the crowd, and the execrations and threats of others who appeared determined that the death penalty should be executed on the prisoner forthwith. The cool, defiant manner of the young Indian who released the captive from the stake, held at bay the more cruel and bloody-minded, who, at a respectful distance, gnashed their teeth and inveighed against the lawless rescue, which the young brave had the temerity to make in the face of the very council that had condemned the prisoner.

Regardless of threats and remonstrances, he caused water to be brought, and the black to be washed from the face and hands of the prisoner, whose clothes were again placed upon him, when the young brave said: "I take this young man to be my brother, in the place of one I lately lost. I loved that brother well, I will love this one too. My old mother will be glad when I tell her that I have brought her a son, in place of the dear departed one. We want no more victims. The burning of red-head' ought to satisfy us. These innocent young men do not merit such a cruel fate. I would rather die myself than see this adopted brother burnt at the stake."

A loud enthusiastic shout of approbation showed that the young Shawnee had triumphed, while the more ruthless shrunk back from the lightning of his eye, which flashed defiance at all who chose to demur to his conduct on the occasion. He thought that a proper courtesy had not been shown to his father's claim to the young man he had captured. Some were in favor of re-assembling the council and reconsidering the vote that sentenced the prisoners to the stake ; while others, constituting a large majority, thought such action unnecessary, as the decree had been virtually revoked by what had transpired, with the concurrence of an overwhelming majority: who were won by the address and intrepid daring of the young brave, whose love for his lost brother had caused him to peril his own life to gain a substitute for the loved and lost.

This sudden and unexpected change in affairs, although it resulted in the rescue of the prisoners from a cruel death, nevertheless produced some discord among the different tribes composing the party, some of whom abandoned the trip to Detroit, others returned to Wa-puc-ca-nat-ta, a few turned their course towards the Mississinnewa, and the Wabash towns, while a portion continued on to Detroit. Holman was taken back to Wa-puc-ca-nat-ta, where he remained the most of the time during his captivity. Rue was taken first to the Mississinnewa, then to the Wabash towns. Two years of his eventful captivity were spent in that region of country watered by the Wabash and Illinois rivers and their tributaries. He gave accurate descriptions of many localities along these rivers after a lapse of over fifty years. The mouth of Tippecanoe River; the Wea Town, and Prairie; Black Rock; the mouth of Big Pine Creek, whose steep rocky banks presented, in many places, overhanging cliffs, crowned with lofty evergreen pines, were frequently alluded to in his descriptions of the Wabash country. Lake Peoria, on the Illinois river, at the upper end of the present city of Peoria, and the Kankakee swamps were also frequently spoken of in his descriptions of the West The great natural meadows—prairie—described by the prisoners after their return from captivity, which they represented as resembling large open fields, extending as far as the eye could reach, without a tree, stump, or shrub of any kind : covered in summer with a rich carpet of grass, and flowers, and often with herds of grazing Buffaloes, were regarded as of the Arabian Nights class of stories : it being impossible for those who have never seen these beautiful and extensive plains, to imagine how they would look.

The last few months of Rue's captivity were spent at Detroit. I shall not attempt to give a full description of the various incidents of his long and painful captivity, which lasted three years and a half, and was terminated in the following manner : Rue and two of his fellow captives whose names are not recollected with sufficient certainty to give them a place in these pages, come to the conclusion to make their escape, if possible. In anticipation of such an attempt, they had for some time been secretly preparing for their departure. At the time there were three or four different tribes of Indians assembled at the Trading House on the Lake shore near Detroit. A circumstance occurred during the drunken revels of the Indians which produced great excitement. One of the Indians lost a purse containing some ninety dollars in silver. Search was instituted in vain for the lost treasure.—

Who was the thief? Various were the conjectures, and insinuations of the exasperated tribes, who were about to make it assume a national character, when it was announced that there was a Sooth-sayer, or Prophet present, who belonged to another tribe from either of those who were disputing about the lost treasure, who, by conjuration, could detect the thief; and tell where the lost money was secreted, which stopped all wrangling, until the learned seer had tried his arts of necromancy. The professor of the black art, looking as solemn as an owl, unrolled a deer-skin upon the ground, with the flesh side up. He then drew from his belt a little bag of fine sand, which he emptied upon the deer-skin.— With a magic wand about the size and length of an ordinary rifle ram-rod, he spread the sand smoothly over the whole surface of the skin. The eager and deeply interested crowd with a solemn awe depicted in their countenances, encircled the magician, and awaited with breathless silence the result of his divination.— Meanwhile the Prophet, as he was termed, silently gazed at the glittering surface of the sand for many minutes, without any definite result. Then after muttering over some half articulated spell-words, and looking awfully wise, he took another long, steady gaze into the sand. Ureka! Ureka were not the words uttered by the venerable seer, but he said, "I see the thief, and the stolen treasure." "Who is he? Who?" shouted a dozen voices—"tell his name, point him out, be it whomsoever it may." But the Prophet, feeling bound by a proper spirit of philanthropy for his red brethren, and deeming that the disclosure might lead to the extermination of a tribe, or perhaps two or three tribes, before the matter ended, gravely declared the impropriety of divulging a fact that might terminate so disastrously. He exonerated all those who had been charged with the theft, and said that the lost money had been taken and carried away by a member of a different tribe from any of those embroiled in the quarrel. This important announcement quieted the dissentions of those who were contending, and restored harmony and friendship among those who, but a few hours before, were ready to use the knife and tomahawk upon each other.

Rue and his comrades being witnesses of this display of the Prophet's professional skill, concluded at the first convenient opportunity to interrogate him in regard to the number, age, sex, and condition of their respective families at home ; and whether they were all still alive, and resided where they did when they were captured.

A private chance occurred within a few days afterwards, the fee was agreed upon and paid, and the three prisoners and the seer seated themselves around the outspread deer-skin, covered with the enchanted sand. After a long silence, during which the Prophet looked steadily into the sand, he remarked that he saw Rue's folks passing about through the door-yard, giving the number of males and females, and their age and appearance with such accuracy that Rue at once considered him a genuine wizzard.— The conjurer then lifted his eyes from the sand and remarked : "You all intend to make your escape—and you will effect it soon." Then gazing into the sand he continued : "You will meet with many trials and hardships in passing over so wild a district of country, inhabited by so many hostile nations of Indians. You will almost starve to death ; but about the time you have given up all hope of finding game to sustain you in your famished condition, succour will come when you least expect it. I see dimly the carcass of some wild animal taken as game, what it is I can't clearly see. It will be a masculine of some kind—after that you will find plenty of game, and you will all arrive safely at your homes." They stoutly denied any intention or desire of escaping ; but at the same time told the wizzard that as they had paid him for his professional revelations, that they had implicit confidence that he would not divulge, except to themselves, any shadowings of the future that flitted over his sand-covered deer-skin. The old Prophet, acting upon the principle of letting every one attend to their own business, said nothing about the "coming events which cast their shadows before" in regard to the escape of the prisoners. Whether his silence proceeded from his not wishing to meddle with the determinations of the fates, or from a fear that any revelations he might make, affecting the interests of his patrons who had confided their all to his prophetic skill and honor, might injure his business; or simply from a sense of moral probity, it was difficult to judge.

At length the set time for their departure arrived, and they commenced their dubious journey thro' the wide wilderness, infested with wild beasts, and wild and bloody-minded savages, whose tender mercies, (with a few noble exceptions) they had long since learned were cruel. They knew that as soon as they were missed they would be pursued, and they pushed ahead as fast as possible the whole of the first night, and encamped about day-break, without fire in a thicket, almost surrounded by a swamp. Here they lay concealed the whole day. Having eaten the scanty amount of victuals they had been able to stealthily abstract from the camp the morning they left, they began to feel pressed with hunger, but dare not venture from their concealment. lest they might be discovered and recaptured by the Indians, whom they well knew would hang upon their trail and ferret them out if possible. They saw no game in their swampy retreat, and had they the sound of a gun might disclose their hiding-place. They crawled around and tried to catch some frogs which they saw plunging about in the stagnant waters that surrounded them; but were unable to catch even one frog. At dark they ventured out from their lurking-place, and pursued their perilous journey thro' the woods, guided by the stars, when they shone, and when they were obscured, by the moss that grew on the north side of the trees—a fact well known to all woodsmen. Just before day they found a suitable place to ensconce themselves, where they laid down without striking a fire, weary and hungry. During the night they had made several fruitless efforts to catch rabbits, and other kinds of game that they had started up during their night-ly journey. Although Rue was well acquainted with the country through which they were passing, (having traveled it over and over in company with his adopted brother, who saved him from the stake, and from whom he might have made his escape at different times) and where he might find any quantity of game ; yet he well knew the imminent danger that would attend their appearance at a deer-lick, or fishing-place frequented by the Indians. Well knowing the cunning and persistent efforts that would be put forth by the Indians to retake them, they deemed it rashness in the extreme to fire off their guns, and were determined not to do so, except to prevent starvation. The morning of the third day found them so weak and exhausted by travel and hunger, that it was determined that Rue, who was a good hunter, should venture out in quest of game. He spent the most of the day in hunting but found no game, not even a bird nor a squirrel

to appease their gnawing hunger. By this time they had reached the streams that led into the Wabash river, which Rue knew
abounded with fine fish, but having no fish hooks with them, nor
wire to construct any out of, they deemed it too hazardous to attempt to spear any by torch-light. So they traveled on all that
night without eating, or stopping to rest, but with the returning
beams of the morning they sought a secure hiding-place as usual.
Their hunger now began to become insupportable, and although
the woods and streams showed strong and fresh signs of Indians,
it was determined that Rue, their Nimrod, must go in quest of
game at all hazards. He scoured the woods for miles around, up
hill and down dale, but strange to say, he could find no game of
any description. A jay bird or a wood-pecker would have been a
delicious morsel to these starving fugitives—but birds and beasts
appeared to be, like themselves, hid amidst their woody fastnesses.
About the middle of the afternoon Rue returned to camp, weary,
dejected and luckless. Starvation now stared them in the face.
Had they wandered thus far on their weary march to starve in
the inhospitable wilderness, and their bodies become the food of
the night prowling wolf—whose habits they had recently adopted, at least as far as nocturnal rambling was concerned. At length
another one of the fugitives arose from his prostrate position on
the ground, and said, "Suppose I try my luck, or lack of luck
once more." Then shouldering the best gun in the company, he
walked slowly off, and was soon hid in the darksome forest that
surrounded them. But this persistent effort on the part of
their comrade brought no hope to the minds of Rue and the other
man, who well knew the want of skill on the part of the departed
hunter. But the race is not always to the swift nor the battle to
the strong, which was fully verified by the fact that in less than
three hours after he started from the camp, the amateur hunter
returned tottering under a small three-pronged buck, which
he had killed and partly dressed. As he threw it upon the ground
the words of the conjurer—"It is a masculine—after killing it you
will find plenty of game, and your hardships will mostly be over."
flashed across the mind of Rue, who now felt fully confirmed in
the oracular wisdom of the old Indian, whose prophetic ken had
so far penetrated the future as to see the carcass of that deer,
which was so opportunely killed to save them from death by fam-

9

ine. If it was a mere coincidence, or shrewd guess of the seer, they considered it strange beyond parallel. A fire was soon kindled, and a small portion of the deer was broiled. Tne experience and sound judgment of the prisoners prevented their eating too much of the delicious repast. They now had enough to last them several days, until they could kill more, and the last words of the conjurer threw the rainbow hues of hope over the remainder of their toilsome journey. When night arrived they pursued their journey with renewed strength and courage, carrying with them the fleshy portions of the venison, feeling comparatively safe. Althought they had traveled many miles from where they started, and in all probability were far out of reach of their pursuers, yet they relaxed but little in the prudent course they adopted at the start, of night traveling, and lying by in the daytime, and thus they entirely avoided discovery by the red men of the forest, who thickly inhabited the region through which they had passed. Had they been discovered by the Indians who inhabited the different portions of the country through which they passed, they would most likely not have been recognized as white men, for their dress, gait, manners and general appearance were completely Indian, from the painted feathers and porcupine quills that crowned the turban that encircled their foreheads, to the beads and ribbons that adorned their moccasins, and variegated the fanciful belts that surrounded their waists, bristling with scalping-knife and tomahawk. They found game plenty, and would have had a sufficient quantity of amunition to enable them to supply themselves with provisions to the end of their journey, had not an accident occurred, which reduced them again to a state of great destitution.

On the twentieth day after they made their escape from near Detroit, they struck the Ohio river, about fifty miles above the Falls. The sight of this beautiful river, which they had not seen for over three years, sent a thrill of joy through their bosoms, and they set to work to construct a rude raft out of logs, to bear them down its sparkling current to the village of Louisville, where their toilsome and dangerous journey would be brought to a close. But before they had floated half the way to Louisville their frail raft was dashed to pieces by the white-caps raised by a stiff gale that swept up the river, and the three passengers with their guns, blankets, and provisions were spilt out into the river. With difficulty they reached the Kentucky shore, and crawled up the bank looking, as they afterwards said, like drowned rats. They lost all their guns but one, the whole of their provisions, and the most of their amunition and clothes, In this sad plight they struck out through the woods for Harrodsburgh, where they arrived in safety, greatly fatigued and worn down by their long, perilous, and wearisome journey through the wilderness, and to the surprise and joy of their friends, who had long mourned them as dead.

Edward Holman, Rue's brother-in-law, after a lapse of two years from the time the latter was taken prisoner, concluded he had been murdered by the Indians, proceeded to administer upon Rue's estate, and sold a four acre out-lot, adjoining the village of Louisville, situated not far from where the Court House now stands, at very low figures, and the deed was regularly executed to the purchaser.

On finding his worldly effects all settled up in good faith, and his out-lot improved and occupied by an innocent purchaser, he concluded to take no steps to disturb the premature administration ; and I suppose his numerous descendants and heirs (one of whom is the writer of these pages—Richard Rue being the maternal grandfather of the writer,) feel but little inclined to disturb a proceeding, however extra-judicial, which had been so long acquiesced in by their worthy ancestor. Rue married a relative of George Holman, his companion in captivity ; and was in several campaigns against the Indians, after his escape from captivity.

On the return of Holman's party of Indians to Wa-puc-ca-natta, much dissatisfaction existed in regard to the manner of his release from the sentence of condemnation pronounced against him by the council. Many were in favor of recalling the council, and trying him again; which was finally agreed to, and the young man was again put on trial for his life, with a strong probability of his being again condemned to the stake. Both parties used strenuous efforts, one to condemn, and the other to acquit him.— The votes were counted. The party in favor of the prisoner's acquittal prevailed by a majority of one, and the young captive was again rescued from the stake.

While with the Indians Holman saw them burn Richard Hogeland, a Kentuckian, who was taken prisoner at the defeat of Col. Crawford. They commenced burning him at nine o'clock at night, and continued roasting him until ten o'clock next morning before he expired. During his excruciating tortures he begged for some of them to terminate his life and sufferings with a gun or tomahawk. Finally his cruel tormentors promised they would, and cut several deep gashes in his flesh with their tomahawks, and then shoveled up hot ashes and embers and threw them into the gaping wounds. When dead they stripped off his scalp, cut him to pieces, burnt him to ashes, which they scattered through the town, to expel the evil spirits from it.

About three years and a half after Holman was taken prisoner, there was a cessation of hostilities for about one year. The protracted war had brought great distress upon the Indians, who wished to recruit themselves, and get more trading houses established to furnish them with the necessary supplies. Holman understanding their wishes, proposed if they would send a young Indian with him who knew the way to the Falls of the Ohio, he would make application to a rich uncle of his in Kentucky, from whom they could obtain as much goods as they wanted. Their necessities induced them to comply with Holman's proposal. He in company with another prisoner and a young warrior, started from Wa-puc-ca-nat-ta- for the vicinity of Harrodsburgh, Kentucky. They struck the Ohio river a few miles above Louisville, Ky., where General Clark was then stationed with troops and military stores. On arriving at the river, Holman and his two companions lashed their guns and blankets upon their backs, and taking advantage of the current, swam over to the Kentucky side of the river. They stayed all night with Gen. Clark, at Louisville, who, after learning the object of their mission, told them to call for whatever they wanted to procure the ransom of the two captives. Thus Holman and his fellow captive, for a small sum, paid in powder, lead, salt, handkerchiefs, &c., were ransomed by Gen. Clark, and in a few days Holman met his friend and fellow captive Rue, at Edward Holman's residence, in the vicinity of Harrodsburgh, Ky. Rue had arrived only three days before, and the reader can imagine, better than I can describe, the transports of joy that thrilled the bosoms of those two noble young Kentuckians, on being released from the perils, toils and sufferings of their protracted captivity, and restored to the society of their friends—who were equally delighted with their unexpected return. Rue and Holman were both in one or two campaigns against the Indians, under Gen. Clark, after returning from their captivity.

Both Rue and Holman lived many years in Woodford and Henry counties in Kentucky ; and in the year 1805, they, with their families, removed to Wayne county, Indiana Territory, and settled and lived close neighbors, on the same section of land, the remainder of their lives, about two miles south of where the city of Richmond now stands.

They assisted in the organization of a separate Baptist Church at Elkhorn, of which they continued worthy and useful members as long as they lived, and enjoyed the confidence and good will of all who knew them. The hardships and exposure Rue suffered during his captivity with the Indians, undermined his naturally strong constitution; and for the last twenty-five years of his life, he was so disabled by chronic rheumatism that he could not attend to any kind of manual labor, and for the most of the time was confined to his house and bed. He was gathered to his fathers some fifteen years ago; having lived to see all of a numerous family, mostly daughters, married and settled around him. Holman, who also raised a large family, mostly sons, lived to quite an advanced age, retaining his physical and mental vigor to an astonishing degree, until the last moment of his life. His oldest son, the Hon. Joseph Holman, was a member of the Constitutional Convention that framed the first Constitution of Indiana, in 1816; represented Wayne county in the State Legislature; and was by Gen. Jackson appointed to a place in the Land office at Fort Wayne, and now resides at the old homestead near Richmond. His second son, Rev. Wm. Holman, was for many years Presiding Elder, and Stationed Minister of the M. E. Church at the city of Louisville, Ky. Another son, Washington Holman, represented Miami county in the State Legislature many years since.

Many years after peace had been established, their old Indian relatives, as they called them, were in the habit of paying Rue and Holman annual visits, staying from one to two weeks at a time. I recollect that grandfather and Mr. Holman made a great parade over the old wrinkled Indian men and squaws that visited them; and ordered their ponies to be well cared for. For hours together these old companions of the forest, would sit and converse in broken English, and in the Indian dialect, by signs, motions, looks, and all manner of ways, which used to both astonish and amuse the younger members of the family, who were often called in to light their pipes, and report the condition of the ponies. First at Rue's, then at Holman's, and back again, once or twice during their stay, was the usual order of these periodical visits, which were continued during the lifetime of their Indian relatives. Nothing that Rue or Holman possessed was deemed too good for these guests from the forest, who were always dismissed with the utmost affection, and their ponies were loaded with presents in the shape of tobacco, salt, flour, and other nicknacks. I remember that on witnessing these acts of kindness on the part of my grandfather and Mr. Holman towards these swarthy children of the wilderness, I thought they evinced quite a peculiar taste: very different from mine, and the majority of mankind. But when we reflect that their lives had been spared, and their necessities supplied by these their adopted relatives, to the full extent of their abilities—we are constrained not only to approve, but to admire such demonstrations of gratitude for favors conferred in the hour of extreme need.

Holman departed this life on the 24th day of May, 1859; aged 99 years, 3 months and 13 days, on his farm below Richmond, where he had resided for fifty-four years. He was calm and resigned to the will of his Divine Master. After conversing freely and affectionately with the relatives and friends who surrounded him, he gave directions in regard to his coffin, pall-bearers, and plan of burial, and died without a struggle, closing his own eyes.

CHAPTER XX.

On the 10th day of January, 1834, Maj. C. and myself, according to previous arrangements, set out from Lafayette to explore
that portion of Indiana comprised within the present boundaries
of the counties of Fulton, Pulaski, Marshall, Stark, Kosciosko
and Elkhart.

A journey of one or two hundred miles was not then, as now,
performed in a few hours. It took some forethought and preparation for such a tedious and fatiguing journey in those days.—
Good horses, saddles, and saddle-bags, well stuffed with necessa-
ries for a frontier ranger were carefully provided. The first day
we reached Delphi about 1 o'clock P. M., and stayed over night
at Lockport. The next day we reached Logansport by noon,
and the same night stopped at a farm house some six miles north
of Logansport on the Michigan road: having ridden leisurely and
examined the lands on Eel river for the most of the afternoon—
being "land hunters" on the look out for land to enter. Our
frontier landlord advised us to go on to the Pottowattomie Mills,
erected at the outlet of Lake Manitau, some twenty miles north
of where he lived, and from that point to keep up the Tippecanoe
river to its head near Turkey Creek Prairie.

We followed his directions and took up our lonesome journey
along the frozen Michigan road, which led through a dense continuous forest. In the afternoon we arrived at a Mr. Bozarth's,
near the Pottowattomie mills. His small, double cabin, which

stood near where the town of Rochester now stands, was a welcome sight to us—being the only house we had seen after we started in the morning. Here we stopped for the night, and were well entertained by Mr. Bozarth and his pleasant and interesting family, who, though domiciled in the wilderness, would have graced the better circles of metropolitan life.

After early breakfast we started on our journey, passing the Pottowattomie mills during the first half hour's ride. We stopped for a short time and viewed the celebrated Lake Manitau, or "Devil's Lake," where the Indians averred a huge monster had been seen in the shape of a serpent, which defied all human efforts to snare it. There was a tradition existing among the Pottowattomie Indians that there was a monster in the shape of a serpent existed in this lake long before they crossed the "hard waters of the north."

Their superstitious dread of this lake was such that they would not hunt upon its borders, nor fish in its waters for fear of incurring the anger of the Evil spirit that made its home in this little woodland lake, which is perhaps some three or four miles in length, with a breadth averaging from one-fourth to a half mile, quite irregular, sometimes quite narrow for several hundred yards, resembling a narrow sluggish river, at other places widening into bays, and more extended sheets of water, that reflected sky and forest like a mirror. The appearance of the ground indicated that had originally been much larger, and that its waters had gradually receded; which fact was confirmed by some of the earliest settlers of the neighborhood, who said they had fished years before in portions of the lake which had become partially, or entirely dry land.

When the Government officers were about erecting the Pottowattomie mills, the Indians strenuously objected to the erection of a dam at the outlet of the lake, lest its accumulated waters might disturb and overflow the subterranean chambers of Manitau, and the exasperated demon rush forth from his watery dominions and take indiscriminate vengeance on all those who resided near the sacred lake—and to convince the government officials of the real existence of this monster, and his terrible paroxisms of rage, which were periodical, they stated that at certain seasons of the year, the fishes became so alarmed that they rushed pell

mell to the outlet of the lake in large schools, or shoals, to escape the exasperated monster that threatened their destruction.

I have been informed that Austin W. Morris, who completed
the survey of the lake for the erection of the mills, said that several of his flag-men, while assisting in its survey had become
alarmed and made to shore, declaring that they had seen a monster in the water—and for awhile it was difficult for him to get a
a man to carry the red flag.   Whether they really saw anything
terrible in the water, or their fears were merely the result of an
excited imagination, after hearing the Indian legends, Mr. Morris
never pretended to say.

In confirmation of the tradition above alluded to, in the year
1837, there appeared in the columns of the Logansport Telegraph,
a communication supposed to have been written by our Artist
George Winter, giving a more particular and circumstantial description of the monster from an account given to him by a fishing
party who said they had seen the serpent, which they represented
as being "about sixty feet long, the frontal bone three feet across,
with eyes as large as saucers."

The correspondent's description of the monster produced quite
a sensation among the good people of Logansport and the surrounding country, and a party of fifteen or twenty daring spirits,
including several scientific gentlemen, was formed to go to the
lake, on a certain day, with fishing tackle after the manner of
Barry Cornwall's fisherman, harpoons, spears, &c., to fish out
the Leviathan, Demon, or whatever it might be that by this time
had got a character equal to a first class sea serpent.

A sickly season, combined with other circumstances, prevented
this grand piscatorial enterprize, which had been planned on a
magnificent scale, and publicly advertised throughout the country
for weeks ; and his wonderful snakeship escaped the leviathan
hooks and snares which had been prepared to lift him from his
watery home, and (perhaps) his capacious stuffed skin from being
exhibited by Barnum all over the world.

From Lake Manitau we proceeded on our journey up the Tippecanoe. Our trace passed through the timber land of the Yellow River country—which reminded me of the dense forests of
Hamilton and Boone counties. We were told that we would no
see a house after leaving the mills, except that of Bennack, a half

breed, and one of the head men among the Pottowattomies, at the crossing of Tippecanoe river, until we arrived at McCartney's, an old Indian trader, on Turkey Creek Prairie; but as examining the face of the country, with a view of entering land, was the object of our trip, we had no objection to see it in its primitive grandeur, unmarred and unmolested by the hand of man.

About twelve o'clock we arrived at the crossing of Tippecanoe, about half a mile below Bennack's village Here we alighted and partook of our noon lunch, and examined the ford where our road crossed the river. The ice had melted away from the shore where we were for more than a rod, while the rest of the stream was covered with ice which appeared sufficiently strong to bear up our horses, provided we could get them upon it. As the horse I rode was the lightest, we concluded to lead him in and pass him over first, which was done with much difficulty, as the edge of the ice where the horse first reached it, struck him about the middle of his breast, and he by much urging sprung upon it with a bound. It bore him up, and he was led to the opposite shore. With difficulty we got the Major's horse to the edge of the ice, and after much coaxing and patting upon his head, we got him to make a bound—the ice broke; he made another spring, and it broke again —he made one plunge after another until he broke the ford open from one side of the stream to the other, the Major meanwhile clinging hold of the bridle reins on the upper side to prevent the deep strong current from drawing the horse under the ice. We mounted our horses shivering with cold, and rattling with icicles, and hastened to Bennack's to warm, and dry ourselves and horses. Imagine our surprise and chagrin, when calling at his cabin door for admittance, he, after much delay, cautiously opened the door a few inches only, and asked what we wanted. We told him our sad plight, and that we wished to stop a few minutes to warm by his fire. He made no reply, but immediately closed the door in our face. The Indians peeped out from their wigwams which surrounded Bennack's cabin, with evident surprise and mortification at his want of hospitality. For a moment we thought we would stop at a wigwam and warm by the Indians' camp-fire, but changed our mind, and rode on along the trace to Turkey Creek Prairie, wet, cold, and slightly out of humor.

Late in the evening we arrived at McCartney's, on the south

side of Turkey Creek Prairie, near the cluster of lakes that form the head of Tippecanoe. McCartney had married a daughter of Bennack, and was absent on a trip to Washington City, to procure a patent, as we were informed, for a section of reserve land, which he had married with his "pretty young squaw." Ben. Hurst, Esq., one of Indiana's oldest lawyers, and one of General Harrison's aids at the Battle of Tippecanoe, resided at McCartney's during his absence to Washington, to superintend his business; and to guard his wife Mary from being spirited away by her father, who had become dissatisfied with the match, and declared the marriage a nullity: having been solemnized by an officer of Cass county, on Indian territory, which he insisted was without the jurisdiction of the officer.

We spent two or three days in looking at the country surrounding the big and little Turkey Creek Prairies, and passing over portions of what now lies within the limits of Marshall, Elkhart and Kosciosco counties, then a wild, uncultivated region, which contained fifty Indians for every white man. But few white families had penetrated this frontier region, and the Major and myself concluded that although the land was rich and productive, it was so remote from schools, churches, and other advantages of civilization that we did not feel like pitching our taberacles in that out-of-the-way place. Every day we met with Indians, who were exceedingly friendly, and invariably inquired for Good-ne-tosh (whisky), offering to exchange moccasins, fur skins, or even pay the cash for it. One morning a troop of about twenty squaws and pappooses mounted on ponies followed us for more than a mile, beseeching us for whisky, which was a contraband article, prohibited by law from being bartered to the Indians. In order to get rid of such an escort over the prairies, the Major pulled out a pint flask of whisky from his saddle-bags, (which we had taken along with us to doctor our horses in case they became sick) and held it up as a prize to whoever could ride and take it out of his hand, meanwhile spurring up his horse to a gallop. Helter skelter dashed along the squaws on the ponies to seize the prize, the Major urging up his horse, and the squaws and pappooses goading on their ponies to full speed. One old squaw dashed ahead of the rest and seized the bottle. The rest soon circled around her. She took out the cork and drank our "very good health," and handed it to another until it passed round ; the younger women and children touching it but lightly. The Major told them to pass it around again, which was done, and the empty bottle thrown in the grass. The old squaw thanked us politely for the whisky, and a few crackers we had given to the children, and invited us to their camp about a mile off, which invitation we courteously declined.

The liquor soon made the old woman feel like exhibiting her powers of horsemanship, and after telling the little urchin that rode behind her to "hold fast," dashed off at full speed of her pony, followed by the rest, the children clinging on behind their mothers and aunts, dashed from side to side, up and down, like Gilpin's jugs, as far as we could see them, and their wild halloo rung upon the air for several minutes after they turned into the timber where their village stood.

While at McCartney's we got sight of his "handsome young squaw," of whose beauty we had heard so much. She appeared to be about twenty years of age, of medium stature, thick set, and was handsomely dressed in Indian costume. I have seen many handsomer Indian women, and thought at the time, that her being Bennack's daughter, and owning a section of land, added charms that could not be appreciated by every beholder.

A graphic likeness of Bennack may be seen in a group of portraits of distinguished Chiefs, head men, and warriors of the Pottowattomie nation, in the studio of our able artist George Winter, whose paintings are much admired by all judges of the fine arts. This group of portraits of the chiefs and braves of a once powerful and warlike race, with many landscape views of scenes on the Wabash, and other rare productions of his pencil, are of inestimable value to posterity, on account of their lifelike delineations.

CHAPTER XXI.

STEAMBOAT TRIPS TO LOGANSPORT AND PERU IN 1834–'35—DIFFI-
CULTIES OF NAVIGATION, HOW OVERCOME—AFFRAY AT PERU, AND
THE STEAMER SCIENCE DRIVEN FROM THE WHARF BY THE EXCITED
LABORERS ON THE LINE OF THE CANAL.

Although Lafayette was generally regarded as the head of
steamboat navigation on the Wabash, yet many boats ascended
as high up the river as Delphi, and even higher; and Logansport
and Peru put in their claims for the honor of being *the head of
steamboat navigation.* The merchants of these two last mentioned
towns, having previously had their goods landed at Lafayette and
Delphi, became tired of hauling them in wagons, or conveying
them by keel-boats the balance of the way, were anxious to ship
their goods on boats at Cincinnati, Louisville and Pittsburg, that
would engage to deliver them at the wharves of their respective
towns.

A few light draught steamers were secured, whose masters
promised to gratify those merchants, in case the stage of the wa-
tet permitted when they arrived on the upper Wabash.

During the June freshet in 1834, a little steamer, called the
Republican, advertised that she would leave the wharf at Lafayette for Logansport on a given day. A few of us concluded to
take a pleasure trip on the Republican, and be of the pioneer
steamboat that would land at Logansport, a thriving town situated at the confluence of the Wabash and Eel rivers, in the heart
of a beautiful and fertile region of country. At the hour appointed
the Republican left the landing at Lafayette, under a good head
of steam, and " walked the waters like a thing of life." We

soon passed Cedar Bluffs, Davis' Ferry, the mouths of Wild Cat and Tippecanoe, and began to anticipate a quick and successful trip. But soon after passing the Delphi landing, the boat stuck fast upon a sand-bar, which detained us for several hours. Another and another obstructi on was met with every few miles, which were overcome with much difficulty, labor, and delay. At each successive sand-bar the most of the boat's crew, and many of the passengers got out into the water and lifted at the boat, or pulled upon a large rope that was extended to the shore—an important auxiliary to steam power to propel the vessel over these obstructions. Night overtook us stuck fast upon the bottom of the river below Tipton's port.

"Tired nature's sweet restorer—balmy sleep," re-invigorated all hands for the labors of the following day, which was spent in a similar manner to the afternoon of the day before, in lifting in the water and pulling at the capstan. At length we arrived at Georgetown Rapids, about seven miles below Logansport, which we was informed was the only shoal water we would have before reaching our destination.

Here extraordinary efforts were made to ascend the Rapids.— Col. Pollard and Job B. Eldridge, Esq., of Logansport, who had goods on board, and were both laboring in the water and at the capstan, were particularly anxious that Captain Towe should reach that place, and his boat have the honor and advantage of being the first steamer that had ascended as high as that point, and receive a bonus of several hundred dollars, that had been offered as a premium to the captain of the first steamer that should land at their wharf.

Several days and nights were spent in fruitless attempts to get over the rapids. All hands, except the women, and a few others, were frequently in the water up to their chins, for hours together, endeavoring to lift the boat off the bar. The water fell rapidly, and prevented the boat from either ascending farther up, or returning down the river. While at this place we were visited by several companies of well dressed and fine looking Miami and Pottowattomie Indians, of all ages and sexes, who would sit for hours on the bank admiring the boat, which they greatly desired to see in motion, under a full head of steam. After four days and nights ineffectual efforts to proceed, the boat was abandoned by all except the captain and part of his crew.

Two or three weeks afterwards over a dozen yokes of large oxen were brought down from Logansport, and the Republican was hauled over ripples and sand-bars to Logansport, and the citizens of that place, and the surrounding country had the luxury of a steamboat arrival on the 4th of July, and Captain Towe had the (doubtful) honor of being the commander of the first steamboat that visited Logansport; for it cost him his boat, which bilged soon after its arrival in port, and its hull, years afterwards, might be seen lying sunk to the bottom of the Wabash near its confluence with the waters of Eel river.

During the next summer there was another June freshet in the Wabash, and the steamboat Science was advertised for a trip to Logansport, Peru, and Chief Godfroy's Village above the mouth of the Mississinnewa. The unusually high stage of the river gave fine promise of a successful trip, and some seventy or eighty of the citizens of Lafayette, a majority of whom were ladies, went on board for a pleasure trip up the Wabash. At Delphi and other points along the river, considerable accessions were made to our company. The boat reached Logansport without any difficulty. There was a large increase of passengers from this point. The Tiptons, Lasselles, Durets, Polks, Johnsons, and many others of the old settlers of the town turned out, many of them with their entire families, for a steamboat excursion, to visit the neighboring town of Peru, and their aboriginal neighbors, and valuable customers at Godfroy's Village.

The boat left the wharf at Logansport under a full head of steam, which was considered necessary to carry her over the rapids a short distance above town. Our gallant boat failed to make the ripple—and after puffing and snorting for about two hours without gaining over forty feet, she dropped back to the foot of the rapids, where several hundred of the passengers went ashore to walk round the rapids, and preparations were made for an extra effort to ascend the rapids. Rosin, tar, and sides of bacon were freely cast into the fire, to create more steam, and another longer and stronger effort was made to get over the rapids, but in vain. Several old men, and invalids, and quite a number of ladies remained on board the boat. On this second attempt to get

over the rapids, all of us who remained on the boat were in great
danger of losing our lives. By some means the boat became un-
manageable, and darted in a backward and lateral direction towards an island, swift as the rapid current could carry it. On
seeing this sudden change in the course of the boat, the captain,
mate, and several of the boat's crew leaped overboard with a large
cable in their hands, on witnessing which some of the passengers
cried, "We are all lost!" The women shrieked and clung to
each other and their male friends in knots in different parts of the
ladies' cabin. I remember of saying, "no danger, no danger,"
as I pressed to the door of the ladies' saloon, from which I intended to spring out into the river; but on opening the door, I found
three female acquaintances clinging to my arms and coat skirts, declaring they would go with me, if I left the boat. Quick as elec-
tricity the thought flashed through my mind that it would be impossible for me to swim ashore with so many holding fast to me;
and just at that moment the keel of the boat near the middle
struck upon a stone in the bed of the river, which turned the boat
out into the stream, and she darted like an arrow past the island,
upon which she would have been dashed to pieces, had she not,
providentially, hit upon the stone, to which circumstance the captain attributed the saving of his boat, and perhaps the lives of a
majority of those on board at the time.

After thus narrowly escaping the destruction of his boat, the
captain deemed it prudent to drop down to Logansport again, and
lighten the boat. Over two hundred barrels of flour and salt were
taken off the boat, which laid that night at the landing at Logansport—and one hundred or more of the citizens of Lafayette and
Delphi shared the hospitality of their neighbors at Logansport.—
After all the hotels and boarding houses were filled to overflow-
ing, private houses were thrown open to accommodate those who
could not get lodging on the boat, and next morning scores were
willing to bear witness to the kindness and hospitality of the citizens of Logansport.

After breakfast the most of the passengers walked round the
rapids, and the steamer passed over them the first effort. All
joined in congratulations for the success of the morning, which
was considered a favorable omen for a successful and pleasant trip.
We soon reached Miamisburg and Peru, two little rival towns on

the west bank of the Wabash. Having business with a man who lived a mile or two above Peru, I left the boat, procured a horse, and rode out to transact my business, while the steamboat passed up to the mouth of the Mississinnewa and Godfroy's Village, to receive the congratulations, and premium of the Old Chief, who was highly delighted to receive the visit, and who no doubt well compensated the Captain for his call at his town. I hurried back from the country, and arrived at Peru just as the boat landed on her return from the mouth of the Mississinnewa. I made haste to get on board, and just as I was stepping upon the plank that led on to the boat, a fight or two commenced between a party that came up from Logansport and some Peruvians, which blocked up the gangway so that I could not get on the boat. The excitement ran high throughout the large crowd, and the battle waxed warmer and bloodier. I stood and looked on for several minutes, and was of the opinion that there were at least eight or ten fights all progressing at the same time. The Logansport party was about to prove too hard for their antagonists, who began to sing out for help. There were several hundred Irishmen near at hand, working on the Wabash & Erie Canal, who, observing the foray, and considering it a free fight, could no longer resist the temptation to pitch in; and gathering their picks and spades, they rushed in platoons upon the belligerents, and soon vanquished the party who had proved strongest in the melee, compelling them to betake themselves to the boat, in double-quick time, shouting, "the Greek! the Greek!!" On looking up and down the line of the canal for a mile and a half in either direction, Irish recruits were seen pressing for the scene of action, with picks in their hands, and wrath on their foreheads. "We will sink your d—d dug-out, be jabers!" rung like a knell upon the ears of the astonished boat crew, who at the Captain's command pulled in the plank and pushed off into the river, to keep the enraged Hibernians from demolishing his vessel.

At first the boat dropped slowly along with the current, and the Captain from the hurricane deck motioned for those who had failed to get on board, to follow along the shore, where he would land and take us on, after he got beyond danger from the "Greeks," as the Hoosiers in those days called the Irish. The assailants watched the motions of the Captain, and determining to thwart

10

his purpose, pursued the floating palace along shore for more than a mile, and prevented the landing of the boat. I stood at the wharf with my port-manteau on my arm, a sad spectator of the shifting panorama that was passing before me, in which, for a while I was a figure in the back-ground. At length I was discovered amidst the wreathing, swaying crowd, and recognized as one of the passengers belonging to the boat. A son of Innisfail sung out, "This divil belongs to the boat!" whereupon I was instantly surrounded by more than a score of the exasperated gang, who had arrived too late to get one blow in the fight, and felt like wreaking their disappointed vengeance upon me. One remarked, "I would as lave kill him as a snake," while another muttered out, "and I, too, would as lave kill him as a nager," I told them that it was true that I came up as a passenger on the boat, but that I had no interest in the boat, nor in the belligerents who had occasioned the hub-bub. Angry glances were cast on me, and several persons at different times lifted their picks to dispatch me. I kept pressing gradually towards the hotel, and the augmented crowd kept circling closer around me. At length one of the party said: "It is a shame to impose upon a lame man —see, he limps." In an instant the scene changed—all were for protecting the "poor lame man," and no returning Roman conqueror was ever marched through the streets of the seven-hilled city in greater triumph, than I was marched through the woods by this troop of impulsive Irishmen, to Tarkington's hotel, where myself and five others from Lafayette, two men and three women, were compelled to remain until we could find some way to return home, which was quite a difficult task, as there were no stagecoaches or other public conveyances then running between Peru and Logansport.

I soon learned the cause of the hostility of the Irishmen, and quaked at the thought of the narrow escape I had made. On the Sabbath before my arrival, one Hoosier and two Irishmen were said to have been killed, and several Irishmen wounded, in a fracas which took place a few miles above Peru; and but a few weeks before the Governor of the State ordered General Tipton to call out the militia to suppress the riots that ever and anon disturbed the quiet of the laborers on the line of the canal.

A short time before, James B. Johnson, one of the canal commissioners of the State, was robbed in Peru of between thirty and forty thousand dollars of the public funds, which he carried in a large pair of saddle-bags, for the purpose of paying out to contractors on the canal. The money was taken from the store of a friend and acquaintance of the commissioner, where it had been placed for safe keeping. Suspicion attached to a young man who slept in the store, who had hitherto maintained an unblemished character. The young man appeared to be surprised and mortified that his honesty should be suspected. His conduct was closely watched during the whole of the next day, without observing the least circumstance calculated to strengthen the suspicion. A consultation was held. It was decided that the suspected individual should be arraigned and tried that night before Judge Lynch. Many respectable and influential citizens volunteered to assist in procuring for him a speedy and fair trial. At the hour appointed, the young man was escorted to a thick woods near the edge of the village, and told that unless he confessed his guilt, and gave up the funds, they would bind him to a tree and whip him until he was willing to do so. He still denied his guilt. They tied him to a tree and gave him thirty or forty lashes with a raw hide, well laid on, and asked him if he was willing to confess. He still declared his innocence. They then gave him about a score of additional lashes, which cut deep furrows in his back, the blood following every stroke. The accused then said if they would desist he would show them the lost treasure. They untied him from the tree, and he took them to a bank of earth that had recently been thrown out of the canal, and told them to dig into that bank and they would find the money. They dug and examined the earth carefully, but found no money. He said he must be mistaken in the place. Then he examined up and down the bank of earth for several rods, and selected another spot, which he thought would prove to be the right one. Thus he kept removing from place to place until they became tired of digging, and concluded to resume the whipping process. The crowd told him as it was drawing towards daybreak, and they were satisfied of his guilt beyond a reasonable doubt, they would finish their work at once. So they tied him up for the last time, as they called it, and commenced plying the cow-hide with such earnest that he concluded they had got in a hurry to dispatch him and get him out of the way. He soon cried out, "I now recollect the very spot where the money is concealed, and if you will let me point out the place, and you fail to find the treasure at the designated spot, you may then whip me to death." After a short parley the lynchers took him down, and followed him to a bank of the Wabash river, where he stooped down, and, after scratching awhile in the sand, brought out several large packages of bank bills, on which were the original envelopes. A general joy was felt at the success of the enterprise, which was soon dampened, however, by the reflection that they still had the mangled culprit on their hands, with a strong probability that he would either put the law in force against them, for their high-handed assumption of legal authority, or die from the effects of the severe scourging he had received at their hands. The thief knew that if he lived he would be sure of the State prison, and the lynchers felt satisfied that if the transgressor survived the chastisement, they would be severely handled for the outrage committed by them; and should he die, the consequences might be quite serious to all who aided or abetted in the tragedy.

After a brief conference between the parties, the following compromise was agreed upon: The lynchers agreed to give the felon a horse, saddle and bridle, and one hundred dollars in money, if he would immediately leave the country and never return again, which proposition was gladly accepted by the lacerated criminal, who felt that he could breathe more freely, and perhaps longer, if he could escape from his tormentors; and before the rosy fingers of morning streaked the east, the guilty young man was making his exit out of the country, well assured of the truth of the scriptural declaration—"the way of the transgressor is hard."

Upon counting the money, it was found that a package of five hundred dollars was missing—which it was supposed had been given to some accomplice, or secreted in a different place.

The citizens of Peru were in constant fear that the Irish, who were much more numerous than the citizens of the town, would rise and sack the village, as they had frequently threatened to do, and kill off the inhabitants.

About eleven o'clock one night, while three or four of us were watching by the bedside of John Bush, Esq., who was lying

quite low at Tarkington's hotel, of billious fever, we heard three
or four guns fired in rapid succession, and a cry of "murder!"
"murder!" near a grocery that stood in the woods a short distance from Fullenwider's store. After a brief pause another gun
was fired, and the cry of murder was again resumed, with a volley
of oaths in the Irish brogue. "The Irish have attacked the town
in real earnest," was the voluntary expression of several of the
company. The sick man told a Mr. Jameson, a tall plasterer,
who was one of the watchers, to go into the next room and get
his pistol, which was well loaded. We held a brief council of
war at the front door of the hotel, at which it was decided that
two runners should pass round and wake up the inhabitants of the
village, and request the men generally to rendezvous at Alex.
Wilson's store, bringing their guns and other fighting imple-
ments with them. In a short time thirteen men met in front of
Wilson's store, and immediately elected Alexander Wilson captain (who was afterwards a captain in the war with Mexico), and
Jameson and another man were sent ahead of the main column to
reconnoitre. In a few minutes the scouts returned, with information that the enemy had taken possession of a grocery near
Fullenwider's store. Jameson said that he fell in with one
of the advance guard of the enemy, who had a gun; that he
cocked his pistol and demanded him to surrender; but not being
able to find the trigger of his pistol, he was compelled himself to
retreat. Wilson showed him that he had not fully cocked the
pistol. Elated with this discovery, Jameson was for rushing back
upon his adversary, but the captain prudently restrained his ardor,
and gave command for a general and simultaneous charge of our
forces. At this time Jameson and James Miller, the druggist, an
old acquaintance of mine, told me to go back and take care of
Bush—that it was "no place for a lame man"—that if they were
forced to retreat, I could not run. I insisted on going with the
army, and told them if they expected to run, they had better not
make the charge. At the word "charge," given in a low tone,
our little squad moved forward with guns, pistols, axes and clubs,
while I occupied the position of Marshal Ney in the retreat from
Moscow, bringing up the rear, being unable to keep up with the
main body. The grocery was soon surrounded, and our captain
demanded the enemy to surrender. After a brief parley, two or

three of the insiders came out to agree upon terms of capitulation. As soon as it was discovered who they were that had caused the alarm, our captain's wrath could scarcely be restrained. They were a few drunken revelers of the town, who, to get up an excitement, had fired off guns, cried murder in the Irish brogue, smashed in the windows and doors of the grocery, pounded on empty whiskey barrels with hoop-poles, &c.—all for *fun*. Capt. Wilson felt so indignant at the drunken rowdies, that he pulled off his shot-pouch and hung it upon the muzzle of his gun, which he leaned up against the side of the grocery, and was about to thrash a few of the leaders of the maudlin band.

Next morning a few of the ring-leaders of the bacchanalian band were arrested, tried, mulct in heavy fines, and sent down to Logansport and imprisoned for several weeks—there being no jail in Peru at the time.

Three weeks after leaving Lafayette, to which place I expected to return with the boat, I luckily met with an opportunity of returning, in company with some of Mr. Bush's relatives, who had been attending him during his protracted illness.

CHAPTER XXII.

COLLEGES AT CRAWFORDSVILLE AND GREENCASTLE ORGANIZED— FIRST APPEARANCE OF CHOLERA ON THE WABASH—REMOVAL OF THE INDIANS—DEATHS OF DISTINGUISHED AMERICAN STATESMEN —MISCELLANEOUS ITEMS—CLOSING REMARKS.

The Wabash College, at Crawfordsville, was projected in 1832, under the auspices of the Presbyterian Church. In the Fall of 1833, a Primary Department was organized under the charge of Professor Mills, who ever since has been connected with said College, except one term he served in the office of Superintendent of Public Instruction for this State. The College charter was granted in the Winter of 1833–4. Rev. Elihu Baldwin, pastor of the Seventh Presbyterian Church of New York city, was chosen its first President in December, 1834, with the following faculty and officers, viz: E. O. Hovey, Professor of Rhetoric and Belles Lettres; Caleb Mills, Professor of Languages; John S. Thompson, Professor of Mathematics, and Robert C. Gregory, Esq., Treasurer. Doctor Baldwin was a man of great kindness of heart and urbanity of manners. His style of eloquence was simple, persuasive, charming. His valuable services terminated by death on the 15th day of October, 1840. The students in a body visited him on his death-bed, and when asked, "Have you any message for the students?" his reply was, *"Tell them to seek first the kingdom of God; my heart's desire and prayer to God is, that they may be saved."* These were his last words.

The Indiana Asbury University, at Greencastle, was incorporated January 10, 1837, under the patronage of the Methodist Episcopal Church of the State. The "Preparatory Department" was opened June 5, 1837, Rev. Cyrus Nutt, A. B., Principal. Rev. Matthew Simpson, A. M. (now Bishop Simpson), was elected first President in May, 1839. His associates were Rev. C. Nutt, Professor of Latin and Greek; Rev. J. W. Weakley, A. B., Principal of Preparatory Department; the Trustees named in the act of incorporation were: Robert R. Roberts, John Cowgill, A. C. Stevenson, Wm. H. Thornburgh, William Talbott, Rees Hardesty, Joseph Crow, John W. Osborn, Thomas Robinson, Hiram E. Talbott, James Montgomery, Daniel Sigler, Isaac Watkins, Tarwin W. Cowgill, Wm. Lee, Wm. K. Cooper, Calvin Fletcher, Gamaliel Taylor, Martin M. Ray, Isaac C. Elston, S. C. Leonard. W. W. Hitt, Joseph A. Wright, Tighlman A. Howard, and Jacob Hays.

Several additional Professorships have been added to these Colleges, which have steadily increased in popularity, influence and favor among the people. In almost every State and territory of our beloved Union, and in foreign lands may be found those who look back to these institutions as their *Alma Mater*.

In the year 1840, Mother Theodore, of France, established St. Mary's of the Woods, a Catholic Female Seminary, in Vigo county, about four miles west of Terre Haute. This is a very popular and prosperous institution, and is largely patronized by the Catholics, as well as many Protestants, throughout the western country.

Prior to the year 1830, a Mr. Rapp, from near Pittsburg, Pennsylvania, settled his colony of Harmonites in the town of New Harmony, in Posey county, Indiana. His plans in regard to his society, not succeeding to his wishes, he disposed of his interest in the town to Robert Owen, of Scotland, father of David Dale Owen, our State Geologist, and of Robert Dale Owen, late resident Minister of the United States at Naples, and author of "Footfalls on the Boundaries of Another World."

Mr. Owen used every effort to promote the interest of his common community; but his sanguine hopes were doomed to disappointment. Like the majority of similar associations based upon the common community principle, the New Harmony colony proved a failure, and property in the village greatly depreciated in value. Houses and lots which cost from six to ten hundred dollars, were afterward sold at from two to four hundred dollars, on long credits.

On the 4th day of July, 1826, Ex-Presidents John Adams and Thomas Jefferson passed to the spirit land, while the peans of liberty were echoing throughout the length and breadth of the glorious Republic they assisted to rear. The news of their death was received by the pioneer settlers of Crawfordsville with profound sorrow. Every conversation in regard to the departed patriots and sages, was a eulogy from the hearts of their admiring countrymen.

In September or October of the same year, the celebrated and eccentric preacher, Lorenzo Dow, visited Crawfordsville, and preached several sermons, drawing large audiences. Many anecdotes and sayings of this world-renowned minister, who was of "Methodist warp and Quaker filling," were related many years after his visit to the Wabash country.

On the night of the 12th of November, 1833, the heavens were literally filled with blazing meteors, darting about in every direction from the zenith to the horizon, resembling falling stars, presenting a sublime and terribly grand spectacle. Many thought the day of judgment had come, and that the stars were flying from before the face of the angel that was descending to place one foot upon the sea and the other upon the land, and swear that "Time can be no longer." Serious consequences resulted to many on account of this brilliant display of aerial fire-works. Some, according to accounts given in the newspapers, fainted and fell to the earth, others became insane, and a few sickly and nervous individuals died of the fright produced by this supernal illumination.

The first appearance of the Asiatic cholera on the Wabash, was in the Spring of 1833, when several cases occurred on boats that passed up and down the river. During the Summers of 1849 and 1854, this dreadful malady swept over the land, like an angel of desolation. Almost every town and village along the Wabash, and many localities in the country, were called to mourn the loss of many of their oldest and most worthy citizens. Lafayette, during these two memorable Summers, lost over six hundred of her citizens, mostly adults, among whom were many of her most worthy inhabitants.

In the Summer of 1834, there was a remarkable travel among the grey squirrels. Their appearance was sudden, and in a short time the woods and prairies literally swarmed with them for two or three weeks. Men and boys laid aside their guns, and killed scores of them with clubs, until they became tired of the slaughter —which at first was entered into as a matter of sport, but soon became an urgent business transaction, to protect their growing crops and granaries from the depredations of these hungry invaders; who, like the locusts and frogs of Egypt, were not only a great annoyance, but threatened to destroy the substance of the land.

The establishing of the Branches of the State Bank at Vincennes, Terre Haute, Lafayette, and Fort Wayne, and the opening of the Wabash & Erie canal, gave a new impetus to the business of the Wabash valley, and gave a bright promise of a prosperous future.

During the years of 1835–6, the land speculation ran high throughout every portion of our country, and all the vacant lands were entered either by residents or speculators. The Hon. Henry L. Ellsworth (late deceased), for himself, and as agent for eastern capitalists, swept whole townships at a purchase, situate in Tippecanoe, Fountain, Warren, White, Benton and Jasper counties, in this State, as well as large quantities of land in Illinois, Michigan, Iowa and Wisconsin. The hard times set in shortly after these entries, and the owners, who had to lay out of the interest of the money invested, besides that paid on the taxes of the land, made it for many years a doubtful investment. But the return of prosperous times, and the consequent rise of property, made Mr. Ellsworth and many others of the company immensely rich.

The removal of the Indians west of the Mississippi was a melancholy, but necessary duty. The time having arrived for the emigration of the Pottawatomies, according to the stipulations contained in their treaty with the United States, they evinced that reluctance common among aboriginal tribes, on leaving the homes of their childhood, and the graves of their ancestors. Love of country is a principle planted in the bosoms of all mankind, by the hand of the Creator. The Laplander and the Esquimaux of the frozen North, who feed on seals, moose, and the meat of the polar bear, would not exchange their country for the sunny clime of "Araby the blest." Color and shades of complexion have nothing to do with the heart's best, warmest emotions. Then we should not wonder if the Pottawatomie, on leaving his home on the Wabash, felt as sad as Æschines did when ostracised from his native land, laved by the waters of the classic Scamander; and the noble and eloquent Nas-waw-kay, on leaving the encampment on Crooked creek, felt his banishment as keenly as did Cicero, when thrust from the bosom of his beloved Rome, for which he had spent the best efforts of his life, and for whom he died.

In July, 1837, Col. Abel C. Pepper convened the Pottawatomie nation of Indians at Lake Ke-waw-nay, for the purpose of removing them west of the Mississippi. That Fall a small party of some eighty or ninety Pottawatomies was conducted west of the Mississippi river by George Proffit, Esq. Among the number were Ke-waw-nay, Ne-bash, Nas-waw-kay, Pash-po-ho, and many other leading men of the nation.

The regular emigration of the Pottawatomies, took place under Col. Pepper and Gen. Tipton, in the Summer of 1838. Hearing that this large emigration; which consisted of about one thousand of all ages and sexes, would pass within eight or nine miles west of Lafayette, a few of us procured horses and rode over to see the retiring band, as they reluctantly wended their way toward the setting sun. It was a sad and mournful spectacle to witness these children of the forest slowly retiring from the home of their childhood, that contained not only the graves of their revered ancestors, but many endearing scenes to which their memories would ever recur as sunny spots along their pathway through the wilderness. They felt that they were bidding farewell to the hills, valleys and streams of their infancy; the more exciting hunting grounds of their advanced youth; as well as the stern and bloody battle fields, where they had contended in riper manhood, on which they had received wounds, and where many of their friends and loved relatives had fallen, covered with gore and with glory. All these they were leaving behind them to be desecrated by the plowshare of the white man. As they cast mournful glances back toward these loved scenes that were rapidly fading in the distance, tears fell from the cheek of the downcast warrior, old men trembled, matrons wept, the swarthy maiden's cheek turned pale, and sighs and half-suppressed sobs escaped from the motley groups as they passed along, some on foot, some on horseback, and others in wagons—sad as a funeral procession. I saw several of the aged warriors casting glances toward the sky, as if they were imploring aid from the spirits of their departed heroes, who were looking down upon them from the clouds, or from the Great Spirit, who would ultimately redress the wrongs of the red man, whose broken bow had fallen from his hand, and whose sad heart was bleeding within him.

Ever and anon, one of the party would start out into the brush, and break back to their old encampments on Eel river, and on the Tippecanoe—declaring that they would rather die than be banished from their country. Thus scores of discontented emigrants returned from different points on their journey, and it was several years before they could be induced to join their countrymen west of the Mississippi.

Several years after the removal of the Pottawatomies, the Miami nation was removed to their western home, by coercive means, under an escort of United States troops. They were a proud and once powerful nation; but at the time of their removal were far inferior, in point of numbers, to their Pottawatomie guests, whom they had permitted to settle and hunt upon their lands, and fish in their lakes and rivers, after they had been driven southward by powerful and warlike tribes, who inhabited the shores of the northern lakes.

The news of the death of General William H. Harrison, within one month after he had been inaugurated President of the United States, to which office he had been called as if by acclamation, cast a deep gloom over the whole Republic, and the nation was mantled in mourning. The general grief was universal. Funeral processions and ceremonies were inaugurated all over the land; and orations were delivered, and eulogies pronounced, in every city and hamlet from the Balize to the Penobscot. As Indiana had been the theatre of the early struggles and most valuable services of the departed chieftain, and Tippecanoe county contained a glorious battle field, consecrated by the blood of fallen patriots, that had been won by him and his gallant compeers—it was deemed but meet and right that the citizens of Lafayette should join in solemn ceremonies, that would evince their sorrow for the great national bereavement. A meeting was called, committees were appointed, a day was fixed for the assemblage of the citizens, the order of procession was arranged, and on the 17th day of April, 1841, the Hon. Albert S. White delivered an able and eloquent oration, in which he reviewed the life, character and eminent services of the departed statesman; whose memory will be cherished by every patriot throughout the land, and more especially the people of the northwestern territory, which sprang into States under his wise guidance.

In less than five years after the death of General Harrison, the nation was again called to mourn the death of Ex-President Andrew Jackson, whose name will ever occupy a bright page in the civil and military history of his country. He was alike distinguished for his bold, decisive and energetic character, in the cabinet and in the field. A public meeting of the citizens of Tippecanoe county was held, at which preparations were made for an appropriate observance of the funeral obsequies of the Hero of New Orleans; and on the 28th day of June, 1845, George Van Santvoord, Esq., delivered an able eulogy on the life, character and public services of the deceased, which was listened to with profound attention by a large audience, composed of members of all parties, who assembled to pay the last tribute of respect to the memory of the departed hero.

The death of John Quincy Adams, Ex-President of the United States, on the 23d day of February, 1848, afforded another occasion for the profound sorrow of the citizens of our Republic, and the world. This patriot, statesman and diplomatist enjoyed the confidence and esteem of all parties in this country, in whose service he had spent his long, useful and eventful life. On the 1st day of April, 1848, the Hon. Godlove S. Orth, by request of a committee appointed at a public meeting, delivered before an immense concourse of people, an appropriate and eloquent eulogium on the life and character of the "old man eloquent," which was responded to by unmistakeable evidences of the deep sympathies of the vast assemblage, who keenly felt that one of the brightest stars in our political firmament had set. This great national calamity was soon followed by the death of Gen. Zachary Taylor, the hero of Palo Alto and Buena Vista, shortly after being called to the highest office in the gift of his grateful countrymen, and the death of Ex-President James K. Polk—whose departures to the spirit world were appropriately celebrated all over the nation. Robert Jones, Jr., pronounced a eulogy upon Zachary Taylor, which met with a hearty response in the bosoms of all who heard him.

While on the subject of national bereavements, it would be an unpardonable omission, were I not to notice the death of Henry Clay, the world-renowned orator, patriot and philanthropist, who died June 29, 1852. Never did the heart of our great Republic feel a deeper wound, than when this colossal statesman descended to his grave. The whole nation was shrouded in the deepest mourning. John A. Wilstach, Esq., selected for the purpose, pronounced an eloquent oration on the life, character and public services of the Sage of Ashland, at Johnson's Grove, on the 17th day of July, 1852, to the citizens of Lafayette and surrounding country. The concourse was large and attentive, and were anxious to treasure up every syllable that fell from the lips of the speaker, who on the occasion seemed to catch the mantle of inspiration from the great subject of his eulogy, whose glowing eloquence had often fired the hearts of his countrymen, inciting them to noble, patriotic and generous deeds. When Greece was bleeding at every pore, and the haughty Turks, who had taken possession of the tomb of our Savior, and the graves of the prophets, were over-running that "land of science and of song," where Plato dwelt, and where Homer sung; and again, when Simon Bolivar sought to form a nebula of free States in the sister Republic of Mexico—Clay's clarion voice was heard in the councils of our nation, in behalf of the bleeding, suffering Greeks, and the benighted, struggling sons of the land of the Aztecs and Montezuma. As long as eloquence, patriotism, genius, and merit are admired among mankind, the name of Clay will rank with that of Demosthenes, Cicero, Aristides, Cyrus and Solon of ancient times; and Washington, Jefferson, Adams, and that galaxy of American statesmen, which has descended beneath the verge of time's horizon, but which still reflects back the glory of the undying virtues of each departed patriot upon the land he so dearly loved.

I would gladly furnish the reader with extracts from the several funeral orations above alluded to, did not the restricted limits of these pages, which are fast drawing to a close, forbid it. But the names and the deeds of these eminent and departed statesmen have long since been woven into the woof of history, and like the radiance of so many brilliant stars, will continue to shine on, with undiminished lustre, until the angel of God shall sound the dismissal of time.

I would here also state, that from the fact that Vincennes is the oldest settled portion of the Wabash valley, and its minutely given history has been in many published works, with which the public are familiar, I have omitted to incorporate in these "Recollections" the history of that ancient town, which has been the theatre of many a battle, and thrilling incident, alluded to in the Western Annals, Dillon's History of Indiana, and the writings of Judge Law, whose facilities for correct information in regard to the history of that city, and of the lower Wabash country, have been unequalled.

As I approach the close of my task, I regret that a want of space prevents me from drawing the contrast between the past and the present, and showing the reader the vast changes that have taken place in the appearance, condition and prospects of the Wabash valley within the last thirty years. I have mostly confined my "Recollections" to the eastern or Indiana side of the Wabash river, with which I have been much the best acquainted, and will leave the Illinois side to the pen of one of its resident citizens, who is more familiar with the persons and incidents connected with the early settlement of the eastern portion of Illinois. Nothing but a knowledge that the few remaining paragraphs will not permit, prevents me from attempting to give a hurried view of the present prosperous condition of the Wabash country, and pointing to those prospective advantages which will be the inevitable result of the further development of its vast resources. Thus far I have confined my remarks to the "day of small things"—the planting of the acorn, and rearing the tender sapling. I now fain would point the reader to the large oak, with its huge trunk and wide-spread branches, towering toward the clouds. And in addition to the few old settlers, with their log cabins and small farms, interspersed through dense forests, and along the edges of wide prairies, I would invoke the magic spirit of modern progress and improvement, and exhibit a land teeming with an active, thrifty and happy population, who have made the "solitary places glad," and carried genius, learning and refinement throughout a land lately occupied by savages and wild beasts. Fruitful fields, smiling orchards, and splendid and comfortable dwellings, have sprung up on hill-top and in valley, where but lately the lone owl hooted in daylight, and the wandering Indian built his camp fire by the sequestered stream, or distant buffalo trace, and poured on the ear of solitude the rude war-song of his sires.

Cities, villages, and densely populated neighborhoods, with their temples of justice, learning and religion, smile throughout the length and breadth of our fertile and beautiful valley. And as I am about to take my leave of the few old settlers who still remain among us, and the sons, grandsons, and relatives of those who have passed from the stage of action, I regret that I have not been able to present you with a more acceptable offering. And to my many friends and acquaintances, whose more recent residence in the country has prevented their names from appearing in these chronicles, I would say, your merit is acknowledged, your kindness and worth are fully appreciated, and I promise you a seat at the next table, should I ever spread another of similar viands before the public. Then will appear a daguerreotype of those able and distinguished ministers, physicians, attorneys, farmers, mechanics, merchants and citizens generally, many of whose names I can scarcely forbear giving, who will then have ripened into old settlers, and be entitled to all the privileges and immunities of that honorable fraternity.

To any of the old settlers whose names may not be mentioned in these pages, I would say, that the non-appearance of your name is the result rather of necessity than of design. And to others, who may think they would have selected other materials from the field I have passed over, and treated their subjects in a different manner, I would say, we are apt to see things differently from different stand-points, and are quite prone to give a description of them in our own way. When you go into a garden of rich and rare flowers to pluck and wreathe a garland, you select with care from the vast variety, so as to combine colors, fragrance, leaves, cups, stems and petals to the best advantage, without attempting to gather and carry all the flowers of the garden in your boquet. It is a chaplet, not a sheaf, that you bind and combine according to the best of your taste and skill.

In early Spring, it would not be difficult to describe the opening buds and flowers that surround our dwellings, or spring up along our pathways by streamlets, and along the sunny side of the hills; but after this genial season has farther advanced, and the thickened herbage and flowers have invested the landscape with their variegated and numberless beauties—then it is that we feel it impossible for us to keep pace in our description with the unfolding glories of that exuberant vegetation that mantles the green earth. So it is in regard to the first settlement of a new country. We may allude to a few of the first settlers, whose log cabins, at wide intervals, dot forests and prairies; but when wave after wave of emigration has for years poured a steady current of population into the bosom of those forests and prairies, we then feel utterly unable to delineate the constantly recurring changes, and give a portrait of the condition and appearance of the country.

THE END.